Table of Contents

Introduction 5
Preschoolers 6

Old Testament 7

God Created Day and Night 8
The Sun and the Moon 8
It Is Good, It Is Good 9
God Created Seeds 10
Sun, Moon, Stars 11
All Kinds of Creatures 13
God Made Things That Fly 14
God Created Animals 15
In God's Image 16
The Bible Tells Me 16
Adam and Eve 17
Adam 'n Eve March 17
Naming the Animals 19
Noah's Very Big Boat 21
Two by Two 22
Dream, Dream, Dream 23
God Is With Me 24
The New Coat 26
Joseph Shows Love 29
Sister Miriam Watched 30
Who Has the Baby? 31

Little Baby Moses 33
Respect Your Parents 34
A Special Place of Worship 38
Moses, Moses 38
Ruth: A Story of God's Love 39
Very Good Friends 40
Special Friends 40
Queen Esther, Queen Esther 41
God Is Good 42
The Book of Psalms 42
Clap Your Praise 43
Wonderful Things 43
Come, Little Sheep 44
God Is Like a Shepherd 45
O Taste and See 47
Worship the Lord With Joy 48
Sing a New Song 49
Sing Praise to God 49
Praise the Lord! 50
Praise God! 51
Be a Friend 53
For Everything There Is a Season . . . 54
The Seasons 55
An Echo Fish Story 56

New Testament 57
Twinkle, Twinkle 58
Look! 59
Happy Teachings 61
Talking to God 63
Amen, Amen, Amen 64
God Cares 66
Let's Pretend 66
Jesus Heals Peter's Mother-in-law .. 67
Little and Big 69
The Big, Big Windstorm 70
Count and Chant 72
Three Servants 74
The Angel's Message 75
An Angel Came 75
Clippity Clop 76
In the Stable 77
The Stable Song 78
The Shepherds 80
A Special Gift From God 83
Jesus Grew Just Like I Do ... 85
I Am Growing 85
Jesus in the Temple 86
The Big Catch 88
Let's Go Fish 89
A Mighty Soldier 90
Seeds 91
The Good Neighbor 92
Listening to Jesus 95

Fuzzy Wuzzy Was a 96
The Loving Father 98
An Honest Man 100
Two Coins 102
Have You Heard the News? ... 103
Early in the Morning 103
Mary, Mary 104
A Change for Paul 105
A Busy Follower 106
Lydia 107
A Love Letter 109
Christ Strengthens Me 110

Index by Scripture 111
Index by Subject 111
Reproducible Art Index ... 112

Wonder-filled WEEKDAYS

Bible Stories for Christian Preschools

Wonder-filled Weekdays Bible Stories

Copyright © 2000 Abingdon Press

All rights reserved.

No part of this work, EXCEPT PATTERNS AND PAGES COVERED BY THE FOLLOWING NOTICE, may be reproduced or transmitted in any form or by any means, electronic or mechanical, including photocopying and recording, or by any information storage or retrieval system, except as may be expressly permitted by the 1976 Copyright Act or in writing from the publisher. Requests for permission should be addressed in writing to Abingdon Press, 201 Eighth Avenue South, Nashville, TN 37203.

ISBN 0-687-01487-5

Unless otherwise noted, Scripture quotations are from the New Revised Standard Version of the Bible. Copyright © 1989 by the Division of Christian Education of the National Council of the Churches of Christ in the United States of America. Used by permission. All rights reserved.

Scripture quotations identified as *Good News Bible* are from the *Good News Bible: The Bible in Today's English Version*. Old Testament: Copyright © American Bible Society 1976, 1992; New Testament: Copyright © American Bible Society 1966, 1971, 1976, 1992. Used by permission.

The purchaser of this book is entitled to reproduce ANY PATTERN, provided a permission line and copyright notice are included.

Editor: Daphna Flegal
Designed by: Paige Easter
Illustrated by: Robert S. Jones
Cover Photograph: Ron Benedict
Production Editors: Leslie Johnson and Betsi Smith

00 01 02 03 04 05 06 07 08 09—10 9 8 7 6 5 4 3 2 1

MANUFACTURED IN THE UNITED STATES OF AMERICA

Introduction

Overview
Wonder-filled Weekdays Bible Stories for Christian Preschools offers 85 Bible stories and fingerplays designed especially for preschool children to understand and enjoy. Each story introduces a key Bible verse. Many stories include craft activities to help the children experience the Bible story as well as suggestions for movement to involve the children in the Bible story.

Teacher Talk
Wonder-filled Weekdays Bible Stories for Christian Preschools will help the teacher make faith connections with their children. Verbalizing our faith as the children work and play is what gives an ordinary preschool activity a Christian value. Looking at sprouting seeds is not just a science lesson. It is an opportunity to talk about God as Creator and to tell the children the Bible story of the Creation.

Teacher Talk is designed to help the teacher think through the words to say to help children learn about God, Jesus, and our faith in connection to the Bible story. Teacher Talk is included with each Bible story.

The Bible
The Bible is central to our faith and to the stories contained in this book. As you teach your children Bible stories and Bible verses, let them see you handle the Bible. Give the children opportunities to hold the Bible and open its pages. This is the book of our faith. We want to give our children a love for its teachings.

Storytelling
Storytelling is one important way we share our values with our children. Use these tips to make Bible storytelling an enjoyable and memorable experience.
- Practice the story before using it with your children. Make sure you know the motions or how to handle any props.
- Vary your voice. Create excitement by speaking more loudly and quickly. Build suspense by speaking quietly. Pause when you want to emphasize or create a sense of expectation.
- Keep eye contact with your children.
- Show the children the Bible each time you tell a story. Remind the children that these stories are from the Bible.

Adapted from *Don't Just Sit There: Bible Stories That Move You For Ages 3-5*, © 1997 Abingdon Press.

Wonder-filled Weekdays
Wonder-filled Weekdays: 65 Lesson Plans for Christian Preschool Ministries for Fall, Winter, Spring, and Summer are teacher resources containing lesson plans that integrate developmentally appropriate activities with religious development. The Bible stories in *Wonder-filled Weekdays Bible Stories for Christian Preschools* coordinate with the lesson plans in *Wonder-filled Weekdays: 65 Lesson Plans for Christian Preschool Ministries*. You may order these resources through your Christian bookstore.

Fall—082110
Winter—08993X
Spring—089948
Summer—089980

Christian Values
Throughout *Wonder-filled Weekdays Bible Stories for Christian Preschools*, teachers will find Christian values presented. These values include:
We are created in the image of God.
God loves us.
We can love God.
We can love others.
God is always with us.
We can trust God.
God's world is good.
Jesus loves us.
Jesus taught us about God's love.

Preschoolers

Each child in your class is a one-of-a-kind child of God. Each child has his or her own name, background, family situation, and set of experiences. It is important to remember and celebrate the uniqueness of each child. Yet all of these one-of-a-kind children of God have some common needs.

- All children need love.
- All children need a sense of self-worth.
- All children need to feel a sense of accomplishment.
- All children need to have a safe place to be and to express their feelings.
- All children need to be surrounded by adults who love them.
- All children need to experience the love of God.

Preschoolers (children between the ages of 3 and 5) also have some common characteristics.

Their Bodies
- They do not sit still for very long.
- They have lots of energy.
- They enjoy moving (running, galloping, dancing, jumping, hopping).
- They are developing fine motor skills (learning to cut with scissors, learning to handle a ball, learning to tie their shoes).
- They enjoy using their senses (taste, touch, smell, hearing, sight).

Their Minds
- They are learning more and more words.
- They enjoy music.
- They are learning to express their feelings.
- They like to laugh and be silly.
- They enjoy nonsense words.
- They are learning to identify colors, sizes, and shapes.
- They have an unclear understanding of time.
- They have wonderful imaginations.

Their Relationships
- They are beginning to interact with others as they play together.
- They are beginning to understand that other people have feelings.
- They are learning to wait for their turn.
- They can have a hard time leaving parents, especially mother.
- They want to help.
- They love to feel important.

Their Hearts
- They need to handle the Bible and see others handle it.
- They need caring adults who model Christian attitudes and behaviors.
- They need to sing, move to, and say Bible verses.
- They need to hear clear, simple stories from the Bible.
- They can express simple prayers.
- They can experience wonder and awe at God's world.
- They can share food and money and make things for others.
- They can experience belonging at church and preschool.

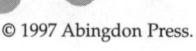

Old Testament

Goals:

1. The children will hear stories from the Old Testament.
2. The children will learn that God created the world.
3. The children will be introduced to Bible heroes and heroines like David and Esther.
4. The children will hear songs of praise from the Psalms.
5. The children will discover how God loved and cared for people in Bible times.
6. The children will discover how God loves and cares for each of us.

The Bible is a collection of stories that tells of God, God's Son, and God's people. The Old Testament introduces us to God and to the many people through whom God chose to work. These people often made mistakes, argued with their brothers or sisters, moved from place to place, and went through many hard times. Yet God loved these people and these people continued to love God. Constantly remind your children that God is always with us and that God always loves us.

God Created Day and Night

by Daphna Flegal

Teacher Talk

God plans for day and night.

The sun shines during the day.

The moon and stars shine during the night.

We thank God for the day.

We thank God for the night.

Emphasize the words printed in bold. Encourage the children to do the motions as suggested.

The Story

In the beginning
God created the heavens and the earth.
The earth was **dark**.
(*Cover eyes with hands.*)

Then God said, "Let there be **light**!"
(*Uncover eyes.*)
And there was light.
And God saw that it was good.

God called the **darkness** night.
(*Cover eyes with hands.*)
God called the **light** day.
(*Uncover eyes.*)

And God said, "Let there be lights in the sky."
God made the sun to shine during the day.
God made the moon and the stars to shine during the night.

God called the **darkness** night.
(*Cover eyes with hands.*)
God called the **light** day.
(*Uncover eyes.*)

And God saw that it was good.

(Based on Genesis 1:1-5.)

© 1996 Cokesbury.

The Sun and the Moon
by Bettye Saunders

God planned the sun to make the day,
And we go out to work and play.
Then when the sun goes out of sight,
God planned the moon to make the night.

(Based on Genesis 1:1-5.)

© 1996 Cokesbury.

Bible Verse
God called the light Day, and the darkness God called Night.
Genesis 1:5, adapted

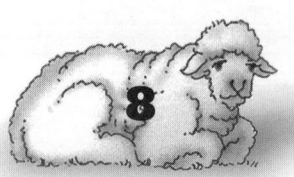

It Is Good, It Is Good

by Daphna Flegal

Encourage the children to do the motions as suggested.

The Story

God created the sky above us:
Blue skies, gray skies, even pink skies.
God created the sky above us.
Sky above us.
(*Reach arms above head.*)
It is good; it is good.

God created the earth below us:
Brown earth, black earth, even red earth.
God created the earth below us.
Sky above us.
(*Reach arms above head.*)
Earth below us.
(*Touch the floor.*)
It is good; it is good.

God created the water around us:
Clear water, blue water, even green water.
God created the water around us.
Sky above us.
(*Reach arms above head.*)
Earth below us.
(*Touch the floor.*)
Water around us.
(*Pretend to swim.*)
It is good; it is good.

(Based on Genesis 1:6-10.)

© 1996 Cokesbury.

Teacher Talk

God created the sky.

God created the earth.

God created the water.

Everything God created is good.

Bible Verse
God spreads clouds over the sky.
Psalm 147:8 Good News Bible, adapted

God Created Seeds

by Daphna Flegal

Teacher Talk

God made seeds.

Plants grow from seeds.

We can plant seeds and help them grow.

There are some seeds that we eat.

We thank God for seeds.

Bible Verse
God commanded, "Let the earth produce all kinds of plants." Genesis 1:11, Good News Bible, adapted

Have the children repeat the phrase, "God created seeds," each time it appears in the story.

The Story

And God said, "Let the earth produce all kinds of plants."
God created seeds.

Dandelion seeds that blow in the wind.
Maple tree seeds that twirl to the ground.
Coconut tree seeds that float in the water.
God created seeds.

Marigold seeds that grow into bright orange flowers.
Sunflower seeds that grow into big yellow flowers.
Bluebell seeds that grow into tiny blue flowers.
God created seeds.

Cactus seeds that grow into prickly green cacti.
Grape seeds that grow into juicy purple grapes.
Pumpkin seeds that grow into round orange pumpkins.
God created seeds.

Apple seeds that grow into apple trees.
Orange seeds that grow into orange trees.
Pear seeds that grow into pear trees.
God created seeds.

Corn seeds that grow into corn stalks.
Bean seeds that grow into bean vines.
Tomato seeds that grow into tomato plants.
God created seeds.

And God said, "Let the earth produce all kinds of plants."

(Based on Genesis 1:11-13.)

© 1996 Cokesbury.

Sun, Moon, Stars

by Sharilyn S. Adair

See-Through Sun, Moon, and Stars

Materials needed: flashlight

Photocopy the sun, moon, and stars page (see page 12). Fold the page in half lengthwise so that the white half of the page is behind the black half. Have a flashlight on hand. Have the children sit down in your story area.

Say: When God was making our beautiful world, God filled the sky with different kinds of lights. Listen to my riddles, and see what I have lighted up. Can you guess each kind of light God made? At the end of each riddle, see if you can all say the name of the light together.

The Story

(*Shine the flashlight behind the shape of the sun.*)
I'm big and round and very bright.
I'm seen by day, but not by night.
When you're outside and having fun,
I shine on you,
For I'm the _____. (*sun*)

(*Shine the flashlight behind the shape of the moon.*)
I'm not as bright or far away.
I shine by night, but not by day.
Sometimes I'm round as a balloon;
Sometimes I'm skinny.
I'm the _____. (*moon*)

(*Shine the flashlight behind the shape of the stars.*)
We twinkle in the nighttime sky.
To see us you must look up high.
We are not planets, such as Mars.
We're little lights.
We are the _____. (*stars*)

God planned for stars and moon and sun
To shine their light for everyone.
When each was working as it should,
God saw that all these lights were good.

(Based on Genesis 1:14-19.)

© 1999 Abingdon Press.

Teacher Talk

God made the sun.

God made the moon and the stars.

The sun, moon, and stars shine on people all over the world.

The sun shines during the day.

The moon and stars shine during the night.

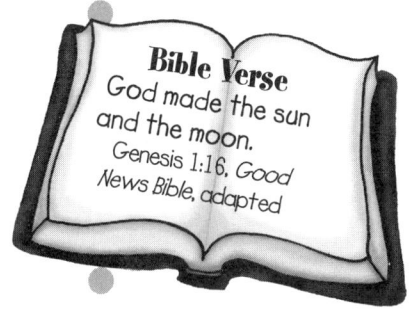

Bible Verse
God made the sun and the moon.
Genesis 1:16, *Good News Bible*, adapted

All Kinds of Creatures

by Daphna Flegal

The Story

So God created all kinds of creatures that live in the water.

All kinds of creatures?
Yes, all kinds of creatures!
Dolphins and whales,
Sharks and swordfish,
Tuna and barracuda.

Is that all the creatures?
No, there are even more!
Sea lions and sea turtles,
Otters and seals,
Alligators and crocodiles.

Is that all the creatures?
No, there are even more!
Starfish and catfish,
Goldfish and jellyfish,
Clown fish and angelfish.

Is that all the creatures?
No, there are even more!
Rainbow trout and flounder,
Salmon and bass,
Minnows and tadpoles.

Is that all the creatures?
No, there are even more!
Crabs and lobsters,
Squid and octopuses,
Shrimp and clams.

Is that all the creatures?
No, there are many, many more!

(Based on Genesis 1:20-23.)

© 1996 Cokesbury.

Teacher Talk

Many different creatures live under the sea.

God created all the animals that live under the water.

We thank God for all the animals that live under the water.

Bible Verse
God said, "Let the water be filled with many kinds of living things."
Genesis 1:20, Good News Bible, adapted

God Made Things That Fly

by Daphna Flegal, Bettye Saunders, Tova Bedolla, Pam Templin, Linda Kandik, and Bonnie Morley

Teacher Talk

God created creatures that fly, such as birds, bees, and butterflies.

God cares for the birds, and God cares for you.

We can thank God for creatures that fly.

Bible Verse
God created all kinds of birds.
Genesis 1:21, Good News Bible, adapted

Encourage the children to do the motions.

The Story

God made the world and the things that fly.
God made the birds and the butterflies.
Flap, flap.
(*Move arms like wings.*)
Clap, clap, clap.
(*Clap hands.*)
Flap, flap.
(*Move arms like wings.*)

God made the fireflies lighting up the sky.
God made the eagles flying up so high.
Flap, flap.
(*Move arms like wings.*)
Clap, clap, clap.
(*Clap hands.*)
Flap, flap.
(*Move arms like wings.*)

God made the bumblebees buzzing all around.
God made the ladybugs flitting to the ground.
Flap, flap.
(*Move arms like wings.*)
Clap, clap, clap.
(*Clap hands.*)
Flap, flap.
(*Move arms like wings.*)

(Based on Genesis 1:20-23.)

© 1996 Cokesbury.

God Created Animals

by Sharilyn S. Adair

Encourage the children to guess the names of the animals you describe.

The Story

In the beginning of everything God made a beautiful world. God made day and night, and they were good. God made the sky and filled it with the sun, moon, and stars, and they were good. God made water and land, and they were good. God covered the land with plants and trees and grasses, and they were good. God filled the water with fishes and sea animals, and the sky with birds. Everything God made was good. But God was not through.

The land did not have creatures on it. God wanted the land to have furry things and slithery things and hairy things. So God made creatures.

One creature that God made was small and gray and furry. It had four tiny feet and whiskers and a long, skinny tail. It scurried through the grass and nibbled on seeds. Can you guess what God made? (*a mouse*) What sound does a mouse make? (*Squeak! Squeak!*)

God made a bigger creature that was furry. It had four feet, floppy ears, a wet nose, and a tail that wagged when the creature was happy. This creature loved to run and to play and to fetch sticks. What did God make that time? (*a dog*) What sound does a dog make? (*Woof! Woof!*)

God made something even bigger. It was hairy, and it had to bend down to eat grass. It gave milk for other animals to drink. This time God made what? (*a cow*) What sound does a cow make? (*Moo! Moo!*)

Then God made something different. God's new creature didn't have feet and legs. It moved by slithering on its belly. Sometimes when this creature didn't move, it looked like a stick on the ground. Now what did God make? (*a snake*) What sound does a snake make? (*Ssss! Ssss!*)

God looked at all the animals, and God saw that they were good. Who would like to make another animal sound for the class to guess which animal? (*Let the children take turns making animal sounds for the class to guess.*)

(Based on Genesis 1:24-25.)

© 1999 Abingdon Press.

Teacher Talk

God made all the animals.

Animals are important to God.

We can help take care of animals in God's world.

God loves you and cares about you even more than the animals.

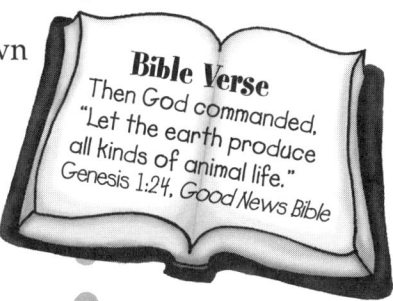

Bible Verse
Then God commanded, "Let the earth produce all kinds of animal life." Genesis 1:24, Good News Bible

In God's Image

by Sharilyn S. Adair

Teacher Talk

God made people.

God made you.

God loves all people.

God wants people to take care of the earth.

Bible Verse
So God created humankind in God's image.
Genesis 1:27, adapted

Say: I want you to help celebrate all the good things made by God. Whenever I talk about things being good, I will stop talking. I want you to clap your hands until I raise my hand and start talking again.

The Story

In the beginning of everything God made a beautiful world. God worked to make the world just right.

God made the sky and filled it with shiny things like the sun, moon, and stars. And those things were good. (*Have the children clap.*)

But God was not through. God made water into oceans and caused land to be separated from the water. And those things were good. (*Have the children clap.*)

But God was not through. God covered the land with green plants and trees and grasses. And those things were good. (*Have the children clap.*)

But God was not through. God filled the water with fish and sea animals and the sky with birds. And those things were good. (*Have the children clap.*)

But God was not through. God filled the land with animals and creepy crawly things. And those things were good. (*Have the children clap.*)

But God was not through. "Something is missing," God said. "I need someone to take care of my world, someone to plant seeds for more plants to grow and to watch over my trees. I need someone to take care of the birds and fish and animals. I need someone (*pause dramatically*) just . . . like . . . me!"

So God made people. God made men and women to take care of the plants and animals and land. God saw everything that was made, especially the people who were made to be like God. And indeed, everything God had made was very, very good. (*Have the children clap their hands for a longer time.*)

(Based on Genesis 1:26-27.)

© 1999 Abingdon Press.

The Bible Tells Me
by Susan Isbell

Have the children say, "And it was very good" when it appears in the poem.

The Bible says God created the world.
And it was very good.
God created the sun for light,
Moon and stars to shine at night.
And it was very good.
God created the land and sky,
Fish that swim and birds that fly.
And it was very good.
God created animals that creep,
Like tigers, snakes, and frogs that leap.
And it was very good.
God created people too,
Boys and girls like me and you.
And it was very good.
The Bible says God created the world.
And it was very good.

(Based on Genesis 1:1-31.)
© 1994 Cokesbury.

Naming the Animals

by Sharilyn S. Adair

Animal Pictures

Materials needed: scissors

Photocopy and cut apart the animal pictures (see page 20). Show each picture. Let the children have fun with the silly names suggested for the animal. Ignore their correct answers at first. After two or three silly suggestions, acknowledge the correct answer they will probably be shouting.

The Story

God made a beautiful world and filled it with animals, birds, and fish, and God made people to care for the world. God asked Adam, the first man, to name the animals.

(*Show the elephant picture.*) Adam saw an animal that looked like this. It was big and gray and had a long trunk for a nose. Look at its big ears. Maybe Adam called it a Bigears. Do you think so? (*Pause for response.*) Or maybe a Lumpty Lump. (*Pause for response.*) A Snogglenose? (*Pause for response.*) Of course, it's an elephant. What a funny name.

(*Show the horse picture.*) Here's another animal. This animal has four strong legs and long hair called a mane. It can run fast. I guess Adam called it a Runamungus. (*Pause.*) No? Maybe it's a Gronk! (*Pause.*) Could it be a Pickle? (*Pause.*) Oh, do you think Adam called it a horse? How silly! A horse!

(*Show the snake picture.*) Look at this one! I bet Adam called it a Stickywick. (*Pause.*) Maybe he called it a Snorfle? (*Pause.*) No? Is it a Borgmeister? (*Pause.*) A snake? Adam sure came up with unusual names, didn't he?

(*Show the cat picture.*) Look at this one. See the pointed ears? This animal has claws. I would call this an Oofda, wouldn't you? (*Pause.*) How about a Snazzle? (*Pause.*) A Pittypaws? (*Pause.*) A cat? Think of that!

(*Show the pig picture.*) I know what this one is. Don't you think Adam called it a Flatnose? (*Pause.*) No? Then it's a Rooter Tooter. (*Pause.*) It's a pig? Wow! That Adam! He came up with some amazing names.

(*Show the giraffe picture.*) Here's one more animal. I think Adam called it a Longneck. (*Pause.*) Is it a Hornkle? (*Pause.*) It's a giraffe? Amazing! Adam really knew how to name animals, didn't he?

All animals, whatever their names, are part of God's beautiful world. When God made them, God saw that they were good. God wants us to care for the world and its creatures.

(Based on Genesis 2:18-20.)

© 1999 Abingdon Press.

Teacher Talk

God made all the animals.

God wants us to take care of animals.

Thank you, God, for animals.

Bible Verse
Good people take care of their animals.
Proverbs 12:10,
Good News Bible

Noah's Very Big Boat

by Susan Isbell

*Have the children repeat the sounds after you each time they appear in the story. As you lead the children in saying, "The very big boat," have them emphasize the word **big**.*

The Story

Zzz, zzz, zzz!
Noah cut the wood.
Wham, wham, wham!
Noah hammered the wood.
Zzz, zzz, zzz!
Wham, wham, wham.
Noah was building a boat.
A very b-i-g boat.

Roar-r-r, roar-r-r.
Qua-a-ck, qua-a-ck.
N-e-i-gh, n-e-i-gh.
Ribbit, ribbit.
The animals came two by two.
The animals went into the boat with Noah and his family.
The very b-i-g boat.

Whoo-o-o, whoo-o-o, whoo-o-o.
The wind blew dark clouds across the sky.
Plip plop, plip plop, plip plop.
It began to rain.
It rained and rained.
The boat began to float on the very deep water.
The very b-i-g boat.

Rock, rock. Rock, rock.
The boat rocked back and forth on the water for a very long time.
Plip plop plip.
Then the rain stopped.
The boat rested on a very tall mountain.
The very b-i-g boat.

Teacher Talk

The Bible tells the story of Noah.

Noah trusted God.

We can trust God to take care of us.

God made the rainbow in the sky.

Noah did what God told him to do.

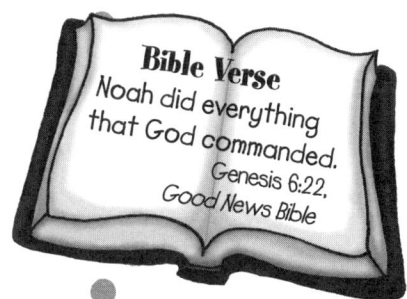

Bible Verse
Noah did everything that God commanded.
Genesis 6:22,
Good News Bible

Roar-r-r, roar-r-r.
Qua-a-ck, qua-a-ck.
N-e-i-gh, n-e-i-gh.
Ribbit, ribbit.
All the animals left the boat.
Noah and his family left the boat.
The very b-i-g boat.

O-o-h, o-o-h, o-o-h.
A bow of colors
 appeared in the sky.
It was a rainbow.
Noah thanked God for
 keeping the animals and
 his family safe on the boat.
The very b-i-g boat.

(Based on Genesis 6:9, 14-16;
7:1-18; 9:13-15.)

© 1997 Cokesbury.

Two by Two
by Susan Isbell
(Have the children repeat the phrases in bold.)

God said to Noah, "What you must do
Is bring in the animals, two by two.
Into the ark bring one and all
Before the rain begins to fall."
Two by two, two by two,
Come into the ark, two by two.

Rabbits and frogs came hippity-hop.
Horses and donkeys came
 clippity-clop.
Humpback camels and monkeys that
 laugh,
Pouched kangaroos and the long-necked
 giraffe.
Two by two, two by two,
Come into the ark, two by two.

Otters and foxes and black and white
 skunks,
And big-eared elephants with long,
 swinging trunks.
Hippos and rhinos and slow-moving
 snails,
And wide-eyed opossums with long,
 hairless tails.
Two by two, two by two,
Come into the ark, two by two.

Lions and tigers, and bears that growl,
Wolves and dogs, and coyotes that howl.
Birds that fly and the waddling duck,
Geese that honk and chickens that cluck.
Two by two, two by two,
Come into the ark, two by two.

"Is everyone here? Is everyone in?
Hurry! It's time for the rain to begin.
God will protect us, me and you,
And all who came in, two by two."

(Based on Genesis 6:19-20.)

© 1997 Cokesbury.

Dream, Dream, Dream
by Daphna Flegal

Rock Pillows

Materials needed: plain paper, crayons, stapler and staples, newspapers or other recycled paper, tape

Give each child two pieces of plain paper. Show the children how to crumple each paper into a ball and smooth the paper flat again. Have the children repeat this process several times. Have the children place their papers flat on the table. Let the children color their papers with crayons. When each child has finished coloring, stack the two papers together, decorated sides out. Staple around three sides of the papers, leaving one side open.

Place newspapers or other recycled paper on the table or floor. Show the children how to tear off sheets of newspaper and crumple them into balls. Have the children stuff the newspaper balls into the pillows. When each pillow is stuffed, staple the fourth side closed. Cover the staples with strips of tape.

Ladder and Angels

Materials needed: tape, glue, magnetic strip, file folder, magnet, scissors

Photocopy the ladder and the angels (see pages 24-25). Cut out the picture of the angels. Tape or glue the ladder onto a file folder. Cut a one-inch piece from a magnetic strip. Glue the strip onto the back of the angels. Place the file folder, angels, and magnet nearby. Have the children stand next to their paper rocks. Encourage the children to do the suggested motions.

Say: Today our Bible story is about a man named Jacob. One day Jacob was going from his home to another city. He traveled all day long. When it was night, Jacob stopped. He found a rock to use as a pillow and went to sleep. Let's pretend that we are traveling with Jacob.

The Story

Jacob was tired. (*Take a deep breath and sigh.*) It had been a long day. He had walked and walked. (*Walk in place.*) Now the sun was going down. Soon it would be dark. Jacob knew it was time to stop and rest. (*Stop walking; stretch arms and yawn.*) He was so tired, he was ready to go to sleep. (*Rub eyes.*) But Jacob was not near a house or an inn. He would have to sleep outside under the starry sky. Jacob stretched out on the ground. (*Sit down.*)

Teacher Talk

The Bible tells the story of a man named Jacob.

God was with Jacob.

God is with us wherever we go.

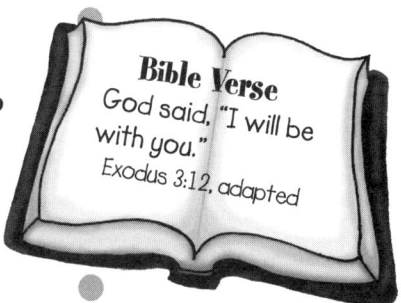

Bible Verse
God said, "I will be with you."
Exodus 3:12, adapted

He put a rock under his head to make a pillow. (*Encourage the children to put their heads on their paper rocks.*) Soon Jacob was asleep.

While Jacob was asleep, he had a dream. He dreamed that he saw a ladder. (*Hold up the file folder to show the children the ladder.*) The bottom of the ladder touched the ground. The top of the ladder went up into the sky. Angels of God were going up and down the ladder. (*Place the angels on the front of the ladder. Hold the magnet at the back of the file folder, catching the angels. Move the magnet up and down over the back of the file folder to move the angels up and down the ladder.*)

Jacob heard God's voice. "I am God. I give you this land. I promise that I will always be with you and your family. Remember, I will be with you."

Then Jacob woke up from his dream. (*Set the file folder aside.*)

"God was here, and I did not know it," said Jacob. "This place is special. From now on I will remember that God is always with me."

(*Hold the file folder with the ladder and angels. Call each child to come one at a time and use the magnet to move the angels up and down the ladder. Say the Bible verse for the child. Have the child repeat the verse after you.*)

(Based on Genesis 28:10-17.)

© 1998 Abingdon Press.

God Is With Me
by Susan Isbell

Have the children say, "God is always with me," when it appears in the poem.

God is with me all through the day,
When I am sleeping, when I'm at play.
God is always with me.

God is with me when I feel sad,
When I feel happy, when I feel mad.
God is always with me.

God is with me when I'm at home,
When I'm at church school hearing this poem.
God is always with me.

Thank you, God, that I can know,
You are with me wherever I go.
God is always with me.

(Based on Genesis 28:15.)

© 1991 Graded Press.

Permission granted to photocopy. © 1998 Abingdon Press.

The New Coat

by Daphna Flegal

Teacher Talk

The Bible tells the story of a young man named Joseph.

God was with Joseph.

God is with us wherever we go.

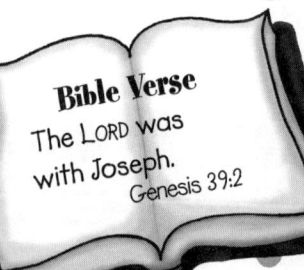

Bible Verse
The LORD was with Joseph.
Genesis 39:2

Robe Shakers

Materials needed: crayons; construction paper in different colors (red, blue, yellow, and green); scissors; tape, glue, or stapler and staples

Photocopy the robe shakers (see page 28). Let the children decorate the robes with crayons. Show the children how to fold the robes along the dotted lines. While the children are coloring, cut one-inch strips from red, blue, yellow, and green construction paper. Make enough strips of each color so that there will be at least two shakers of the same color. If you do not have one of these colors, substitute a different color and substitute that color in the story. Let the children choose one color. Help each child glue, tape, or staple three or four of the same color strips to the bottom of his or her robe. Glue or staple the bottom of the robe together over the strips. Each child should have only one color of strips.

Show the children how to hold the robe part of their shakers. Have the children hold their robe shakers as you tell the story. Each time you name a color, have the children with that color shaker hold up their shakers and wave them in the air.

The Story

"Look at my new coat!" Joseph called to his brothers. He held out his arms in the long sleeves of his coat and turned around.

"It has so many beautiful colors," he said. "It has red (*wave red shakers*) and blue (*wave blue shakers*) and yellow (*wave yellow shakers*) and green (*wave green shakers*) colors."

"Where did you get that coat?" asked one of Joseph's brothers.

"Father gave it to me," answered Joseph.

The brothers were not happy about Joseph's coat. They did not like the beautiful colors.

They did not like the red (*wave red shakers*) and blue (*wave blue shakers*) and yellow (*wave yellow shakers*) and green (*wave green shakers*) colors.

"Father has never given any of us a coat like that," said one brother.

"Father loves Joseph more than he loves us," said another brother. The brothers decided to do something unkind to Joseph. They tore Joseph's coat with its beautiful colors.

They tore the red (*wave red shakers*) and blue (*wave blue shakers*) and yellow (*wave yellow shakers*) and green (*wave green shakers*) colors. Then they pushed Joseph into a big hole.

"Look over there," said one brother. "Do you see that caravan? It's on its way to Egypt."

"Let's sell Joseph to the caravan," said another brother. "They will take him far away to Egypt."

The brothers pulled Joseph out of the hole. Soon Joseph was on his way to Egypt with the caravan. Joseph was afraid, but he remembered his father and the beautiful coat. He remembered the red (*wave red shakers*) and blue (*wave blue shakers*) and yellow (*wave yellow shakers*) and green (*wave green shakers*) colors. Joseph also remembered that God was with him.

When Joseph got to Egypt, he had many adventures. He became an important man in Egypt. One day Joseph's brothers came to Egypt to buy food. The brothers had to buy the food from Joseph. When Joseph saw his brothers, he remembered his beautiful coat. He remembered the red (*wave red shakers*) and blue (*wave blue shakers*) and yellow (*wave yellow shakers*) and green (*wave green shakers*) colors. Joseph also remembered that God was with him.

At first the brothers did not know Joseph because he had grown up and had become an important man. When Joseph told the brothers who he was, they told Joseph that they were sorry that they had been unkind to him. Joseph forgave his brothers.

"God is with me," said Joseph. "I'm glad that I came to live in Egypt."

Joseph gave his brothers the food they needed. Joseph's brothers and Joseph's father came to Egypt to live with Joseph. Joseph was happy to see his father again. He remembered the beautiful coat his father had given him—the coat with the red (*wave red shakers*) and blue (*wave blue shakers*) and yellow (*wave yellow shakers*) and green (*wave green shakers*) colors. Joseph also remembered that God was with him.

(Based on Genesis 37:17-32; 41:39-57; 45:4-5.)

© 1998 Abingdon Press.

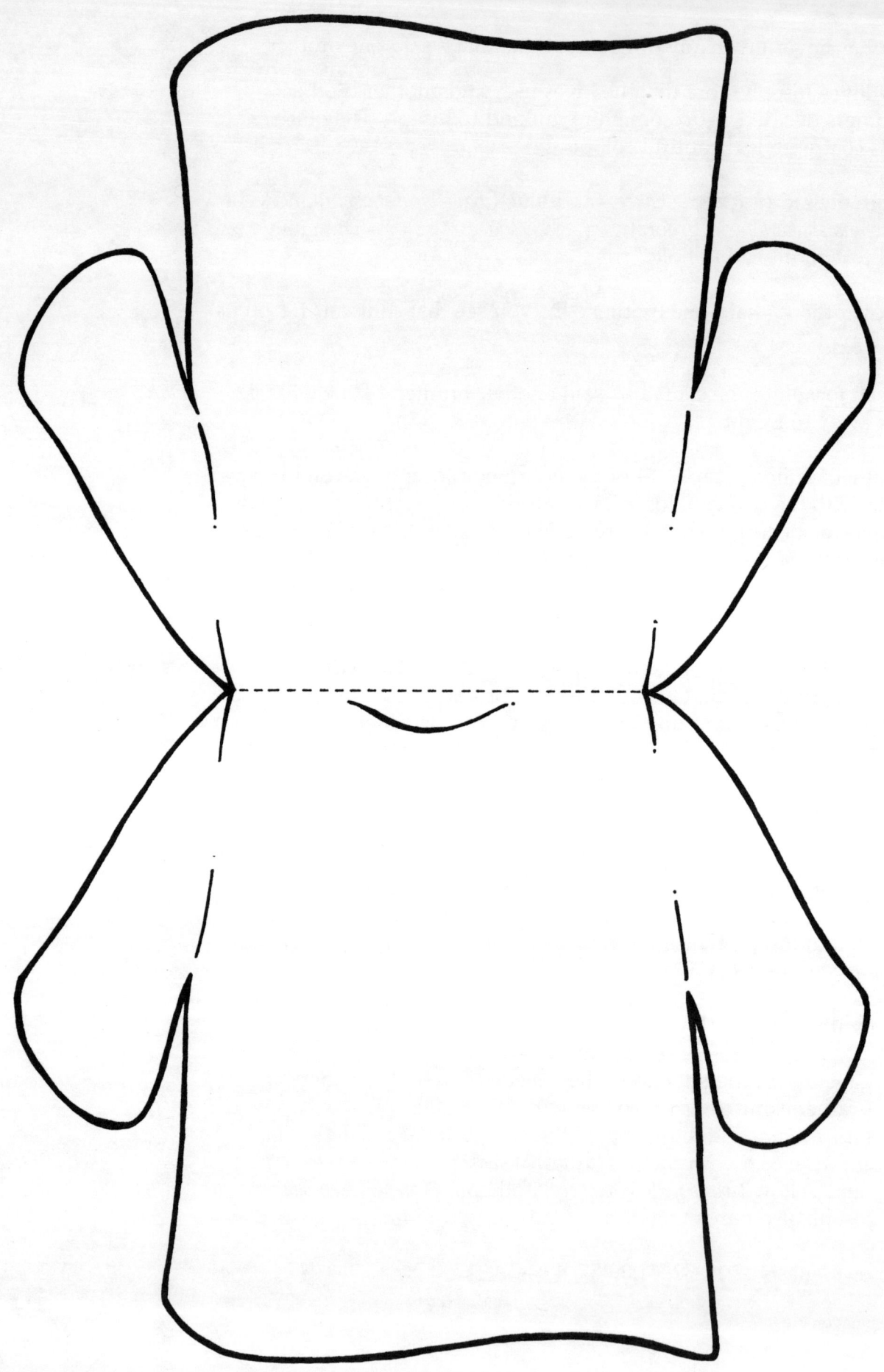

28 Permission granted to photocopy. © 1998 Abingdon Press.

Joseph Shows Love

by Susan Isbell

The Story

When Joseph grew up, he lived in Egypt. Joseph's family did not know he was in Egypt.

Joseph became a favorite helper to the king. One of Joseph's jobs was to make sure there was enough food for the people to eat.

One year there was very little food and water. People were hungry, and crops would not grow. Joseph had planned for just such a time. Joseph had kept enough food so that no one would be hungry.

Joseph's brothers needed food too. Their father, Jacob, sent the brothers to Egypt to ask for food.

When the brothers arrived in Egypt, they went to the man giving out the food. That man was Joseph, their brother! At first they did not know who he was. Joseph looked so different.

Joseph knew his brothers. He remembered how unkind they had been to him. Joseph also remembered his father, Jacob, and how much Jacob loved him. Joseph knew that God wanted him to forgive his brothers and help them.

Joseph gave his brothers food to take back to Jacob and their family. Soon the brothers brought Jacob and the rest of their family to live with Joseph in Egypt.

Joseph forgave his brothers and showed his love for them by giving them food. Joseph knew that God was with him.

(Based on Genesis 41:39-57; 45:4-5.)

© 1994 Cokesbury.

Teacher Talk

The Bible tells us the story of Joseph.

God was with Joseph.

God is with us wherever we go.

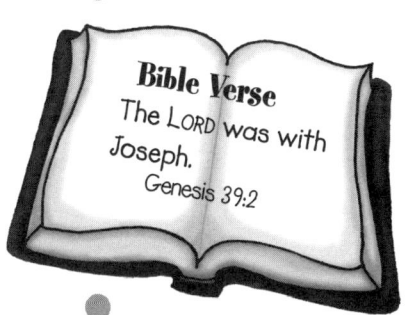

Bible Verse
The LORD was with Joseph.
Genesis 39:2

Sister Miriam Watched

by Daphna Flegal

Teacher Talk

The Bible tells the story of Moses and Miriam.

Miriam and Moses trusted God.

We can show love to our families.

We can trust God to take care of us.

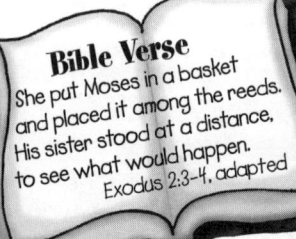

Bible Verse
She put Moses in a basket and placed it among the reeds. His sister stood at a distance, to see what would happen.
Exodus 2:3-4, adapted

Basket

Materials needed: crayons, scissors, tape, baby doll

Photocopy the basket (see page 32). Let the children color their baskets with crayons. Cut the corners of each basket along the lines. Fold up and overlap each corner. Tape each corner together.

Use the basket and a baby doll as you tell this story. Follow the suggestions printed in italics and encourage the children to do the motions with you.

The Story

Rock, rock, rock. (*Rock the doll in your arms. Have each child pretend to rock a baby.*) Mother rocked baby Moses gently in her arms. Then Mother put baby Moses into a basket. (*Put the doll in the basket. Set the basket on the floor.*)

Sister Miriam watched. (*Hold your hands above your eyes.*) She loved baby Moses.

Splash, splash, splash. (*Make rippling motions with your fingers.*) Mother carefully placed the basket at the edge of the river.

Sister Miriam watched. (*Hold your hands above your eyes.*) She knew Mother was hiding baby Moses in the basket to keep him safe from Pharaoh.

Splash, splash, splash. (*Make rippling motions with your fingers.*) The basket floated on the water.

Sister Miriam watched. (*Hold your hands above your eyes.*) She wanted to help keep baby Moses safe. Miriam hid behind the tall grasses at the edge of the river where she could watch baby Moses.

Splash, splash, splash. (*Make rippling motions with your fingers.*) Soon Pharaoh's daughter waded into the river to take a bath.

Sister Miriam watched. (*Hold your hands above your eyes.*) She knew Pharaoh's daughter was a princess.

Splash, splash, splash. (*Make rippling motions with your fingers.*) The princess saw the basket floating on the river.

Sister Miriam watched. (*Hold your hands above your eyes.*) She saw the princess open the basket and find baby Moses.

Splash, splash, splash. (*Make rippling motions with your fingers.*) Miriam waded in the water to the princess. She knew that the princess would keep baby Moses safe from Pharaoh.

"Do you want me to find a woman to feed and help care for the baby?" Miriam asked the princess.

"Yes," said the princess. "Go and find someone."

Splash, splash, splash. (*Make rippling motions with your fingers.*) Miriam waded out of the water. She ran to get Moses' own mother and brought her to the princess.

Rock, rock, rock. (*Rock the baby doll in your arms. Have each child pretend to rock a baby.*) Mother rocked baby Moses gently in her arms once again.

Sister Miriam watched. (*Hold your hands above your eyes.*) She was happy baby Moses would be safe with the princess and Moses' mother.

The princess, Moses' mother, and Miriam loved and cared for Moses as he grew.

(Based on Exodus 2:1-10.)

© 1997 Abingdon Press.

Who Has the Baby?
by Daphna Flegal

Have the children stand in a circle. Place a baby doll in a basket in the middle of the circle. Let one child be Miriam. Have Miriam close her or his eyes. While Miriam isn't looking, choose another child to be the princess. Have the princess quietly take the baby out of the basket. **Say:**

Miriam, Miriam,
Who has the baby?
Guess who it is today.

Miriam, Miriam,
Who has the baby?
Listen to the person say,
"I'm holding baby Moses."

Have the princess repeat, "I'm holding baby Moses." Let Miriam try to guess who is the princess. Continue the game, giving each child an opportunity to be Miriam and the princess.

(Based on Exodus 2:1-10.)

© 1997 Cokesbury.

Little Baby Moses

by Elizabeth Crocker

As you say the poem below, encourage the children to repeat the lines and to do the motions after you.

The Story

Here is baby Moses,
(*Rock your arms in a cradling motion.*)
On the river he will float.
(*Make a gentle motion with your hand, as if on water.*)
For Moses' mother made him
(*Rock your arms in a cradling motion.*)
A little basket boat.
(*Cup your hands to make a "boat."*)

Sister Miriam watched,
(*Place your hands above your eyes as if searching.*)
Until the princess found him there;
(*Look both ways.*)
Then little baby Moses
(*Rock your arms in a cradling motion.*)
Went back to his mother's care.
(*Continue rocking.*)

(Based on Exodus 2:1-10.)

© 1996 Cokesbury.

Teacher Talk

The Bible tells the story of Moses and Miriam.

Miriam and Moses trusted God.

We can show love to our families.

We can trust God to take care of us.

Bible Verse
Moses was born, and he was beautiful before God.
Acts 7:20

Respect Your Parents

by Sharilyn S. Adair

Teacher Talk

God planned for parents.

God created all kinds of families.

We thank God for families.

Bible Verse
Respect your father and your mother.
Exodus 20:12,
Good News Bible

The Ten Commandments

Materials needed: scissors

Photocopy and cut apart the numbers (see pages 36-37) for each child. Give each child a set of numbers. Explain that when you say a number in the story, you will hold up a card with that number on it. The children are to find their copy of that number and hold it up.

The Story

The Hebrew people followed Moses, their leader, into the wilderness. One day they came to a mountain. They put up their tents at the bottom of the mountain.

God said to Moses, "I want the people to know that I am always with them. I want them to be my people. I have some rules that will help them live together. Come to the top of the mountain, and I will give you the rules."

"How many rules are there?" Moses wondered. Moses told the people that God would give them some special rules.

"How many rules are there?" the people wondered. Moses went up the mountain to get the rules.

When Moses brought the rules to the people, they said, "Moses, Moses, is there one rule?" (*Hold up Number 1.*)

Moses said, "There is one rule. It is a good rule. The first rule is 'Love God.'" Then Moses said, "And there are more rules."

"Oh," said the people, "Are there two rules?" (*Hold up Number 2.*)

"There are more than two rules," said Moses.

"Could there be three rules?" asked the people. (*Hold up Number 3.*)

"There are three rules and more," said Moses.

"Then there must be four rules," said the people. (*Hold up Number 4.*)

"More than four," said Moses.

"Perhaps there are five rules," said the people. (*Hold up Number 5.*)

"Rule Number 5 is a good rule to remember. It says, 'Love your father and your mother.' But Number 5 is not the last rule," said Moses.

"Six?" asked the people. (*Hold up Number 6.*)

"Still more," said Moses.

"Seven?" asked the people. (*Hold up Number 7.*)

"There are seven and more," said Moses.

"Are there eight rules?" asked the people. (*Hold up Number 8.*)

"Rule Number 8 is about stealing: 'Do not take anything that doesn't belong to you,'" said Moses. "But Number 8 is not the last rule."

"Then there are nine rules!" the people exclaimed. (*Hold up Number 9.*)

"Nine rules and one to go," said Moses.

"Ten!" shouted the people. (*Hold up Number 10.*) "There are ten rules."

"Yes," said Moses, "Number 10 is the last rule. God has given us ten good rules."

The people were happy that God had given them one (*hold up Number 1*), two (*hold up Number 2*), three (*hold up Number 3*), four (*hold up Number 4*), five (*hold up Number 5*), six (*hold up Number 6*), seven (*hold up Number 7*), eight (*hold up Number 8*), nine (*hold up Number 9*), ten (*hold up Number 10*) good rules.

(Based on Exodus 20:1-17.)

© 1998 Abingdon Press.

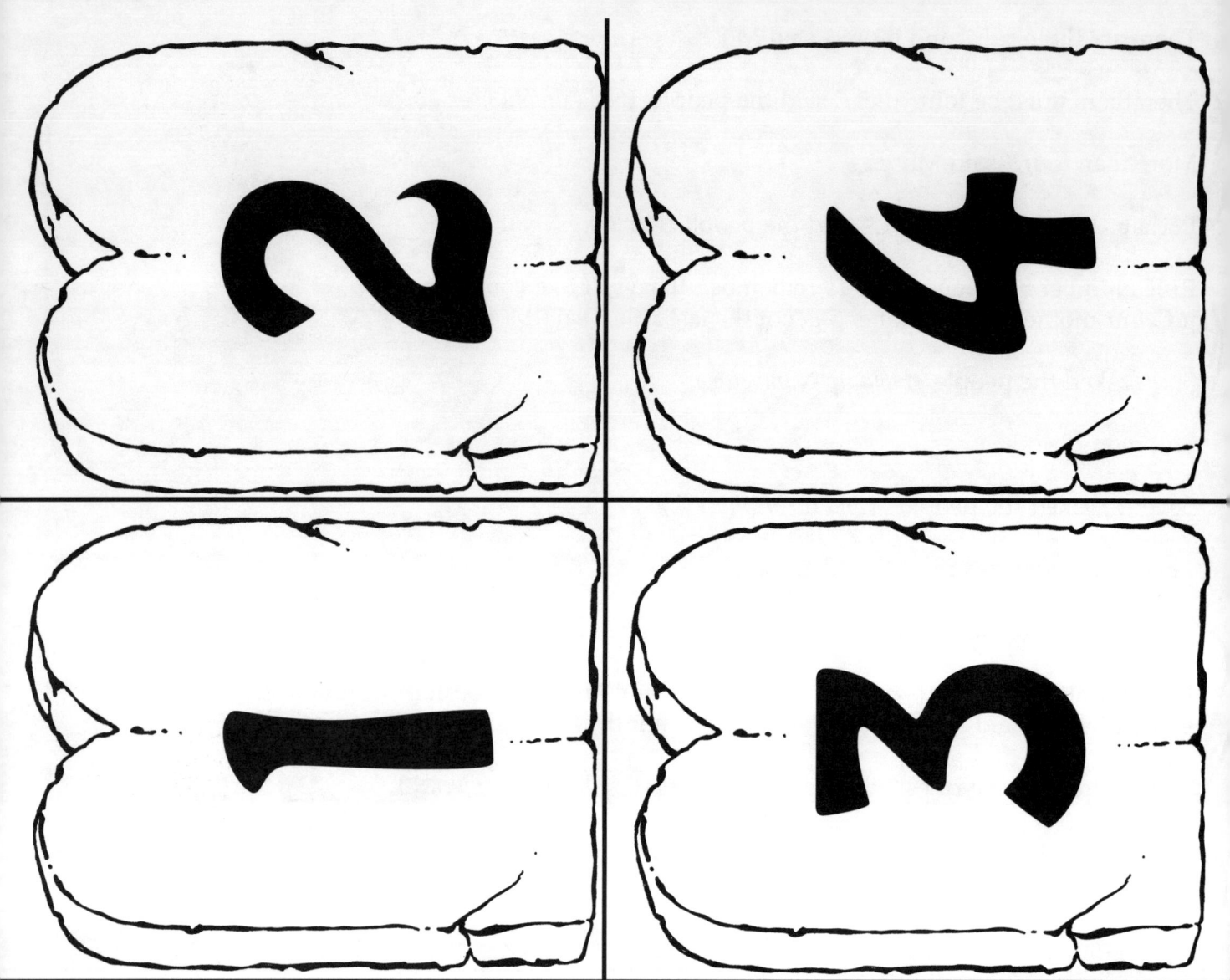

A Special Place of Worship

by Elizabeth Crocker

Teacher Talk

The Bible tells the story of when the people built a beautiful place to worship God.

We are all beautiful to God.

The Story

"Hurry, bring the purple wool! Bring the red and the blue wool too!" said Judith happily. "Moses said that we must bring our gifts to worship God!"

"Yes!" said Machi. "Everyone is bringing a gift!"

Judith and Machi hurried to join the others. Moses told the people what to bring and how they should make the place of worship. They were building a big tent with a special altar. There would be many curtains inside the tent.

"Look!" said Machi. "There is Caleb. He is bringing incense and oil for the lamps!"

"And there is Deborah with her friends!" said Judith. "Look at the jewels they are bringing! We will use them to make special clothes for Aaron, our priest. Look at the silver, gold, and bronze! See how they sparkle in the sun! They will be so beautiful on the altar."

"There is Bezalel (BEZ-uh-lel)!" said Machi. "He and Oholiab (oh-HOH-lee-ab) are bringing wood to make a table for the tent. I will see if I can help. We are making a special place of worship, just the way God told Moses we should!"

(Based on Exodus 25:1-9.)

© 1996 Cokesbury.

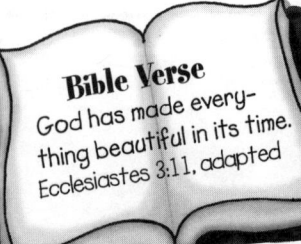

Bible Verse
God has made everything beautiful in its time.
Ecclesiastes 3:11, adapted

Moses, Moses
by Elizabeth Crocker

Moses, Moses,
What gifts should we bring?
For a place to worship,
To praise God and sing?

People, people,
Here's what to bring:
Spices that smell nice,
And shiny gold things.

(Based on Exodus 25:1-9.)

© 1996 Cokesbury.

The Angel's Good News
Luke 1:26-38; Matt. 1:18-25

✧ Folding Angel Picture ✧

God sent an angel to Mary and Joseph with some happy news. First, the angel visited Mary and told her that she was going to have a baby boy. Mary was to name Him "Jesus." Then the angel told Joseph to take care of Mary and the baby.

Mary and Joseph both listened to the angel's good news. They were happy to obey God. We can listen to and obey God, too.

Color the pictures. Your teacher will show you how to cut the pictures to let the angel visit Mary and then Joseph.

(Luke 1:26-38; Matt. 1:18-25)

For the Teacher: Duplicate the page for each child. After the children color, help them cut their pictures on the solid lines and fold the angel back on the broken lines. Show how to make their pictures tell the angel's story. Have the angel first visit Mary, then Joseph. Next, the children can open their pictures to show Mary and Joseph both saying they will obey God. Then they can fold the angel picture back to show the angel returning to heaven.

✧ Find the Bibles ✧

Look for Jesus
Isaiah 7:14; Micah 5:2

Another prophet, Micah, announced that Jesus would be born in the town of Bethlehem. People thought that was odd because Bethlehem was such a small town. But Micah knew he was only announcing what God told him to say. God's Word is always true.

In Old Testament times God spoke to people through the prophets. Today, God speaks to us through the Bible. Color the picture of Bethlehem and see if you can find the five hidden Bibles.

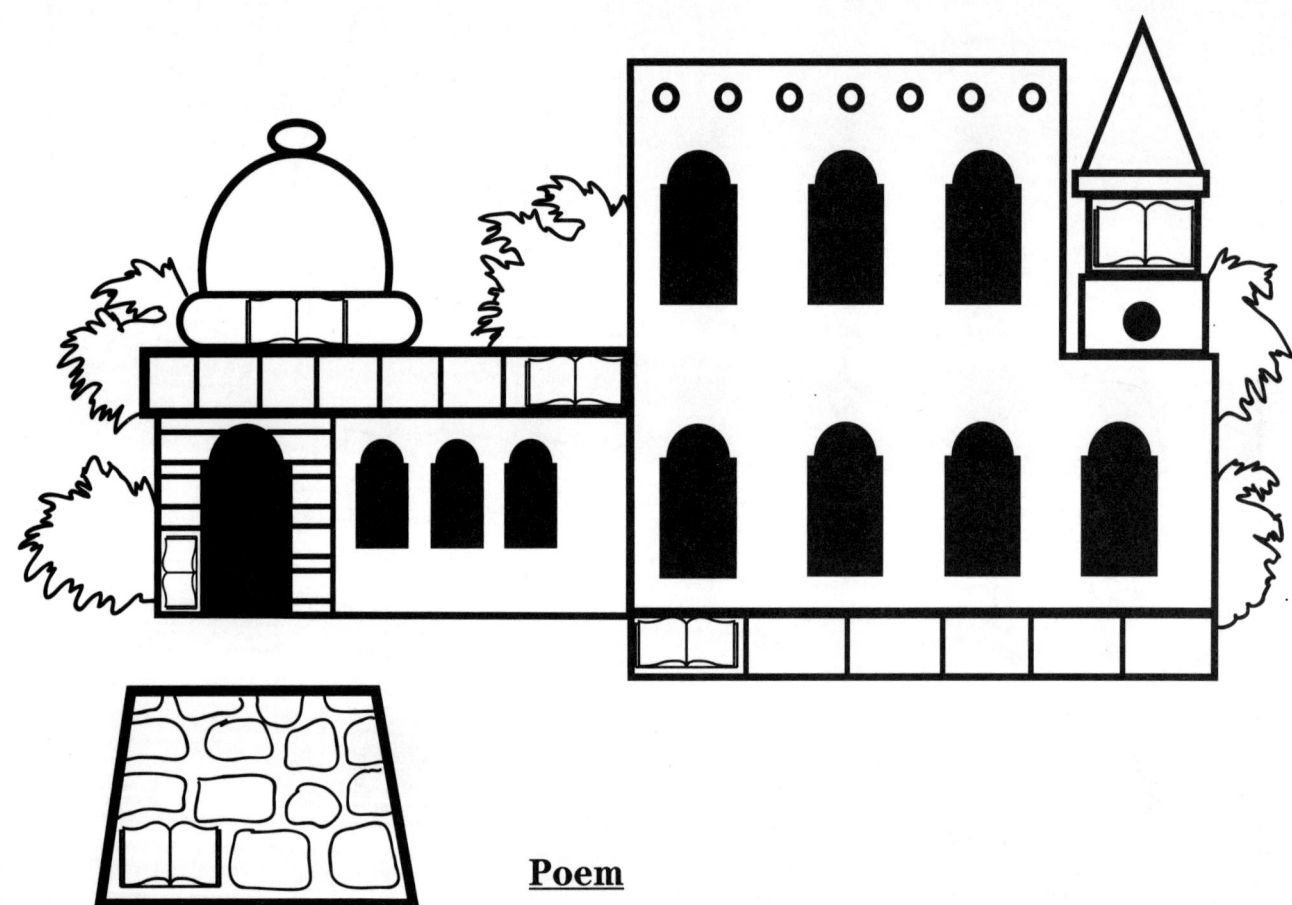

Poem

God spoke to the prophets, their beards long and gray.

He told them just what He wanted them to say.

Today we have the Bible, God's holy Word.

By reading it each day, God's voice is heard.

For the Teacher: Duplicate the page for each child. Assist the children in finding the five hidden Bibles. After they color the picture, say the poem to the children. Have the children stroke their imaginary beards for the first two lines and hold their Bibles for the last two.

Ruth: A Story of God's Love
by Grace Tanner Cook

Have the children stand in a circle. Let the children repeat the words printed in bold and do the suggested motions as you tell the story.

The Story

Splash, splash, splash. (*Pretend to pull a bucket out of a well.*) The water in the bucket splashed as Ruth pulled it from the well. She and her mother-in-law, Naomi, wanted a drink of water.

Naomi smiled at Ruth. "I must return to my relatives in Bethlehem," Naomi said. "You must go back to your family in Moab."

Sob, sob, sob. (*Pretend to rub eyes.*) Tears ran down Ruth's cheeks as she hugged Naomi.

"I love you, Naomi," Ruth cried. "I want to go with you to Bethlehem. I will take care of you there, and I will worship your God."

Step, step, step. (*Walk in place.*) Ruth and Naomi walked to Bethlehem together. When they got there, they had no money to buy food.

Naomi and Ruth were hungry. "Don't worry," Ruth told Naomi. "I will gather grain from the fields. We will make bread."

Scoop, scoop, scoop. (*Pretend to pick up grain.*) Ruth used her hands to scoop grain from the ground to fill her bag. Ruth worked hard all day long.

Boaz saw how hard Ruth worked to gather grain for herself and her mother-in-law, Naomi.

Work, work, work. (*Wipe brow as if hot.*) Ruth worked hard gathering grain.

"Ruth," said Boaz, "you may gather grain from my fields, drink water from my water jars, and eat bread with my workers."

Ruth smiled in surprise. "Thank you for your kindness," she said.

As time went on, Boaz grew to love Ruth, and he married her.

Waa, waa, waa. (*Pretend to rock baby.*) Ruth gave birth to a baby boy named Obed. Ruth, Boaz, and Naomi knew that God had blessed their family.

(Based on Ruth 1–4.)

© 1997 Cokesbury.

Teacher Talk

The Bible tells the story of a woman named Ruth.

God created families to love one another.

We are all a part of God's family.

God loves every person in the world.

We thank God for our family.

Bible Verse
You are members of the family of God.
Ephesians 2:19, Good News Bible, adapted

Very Good Friends
by Daphna Flegal

Teacher Talk

A friend is a gift from God.

I'm glad you're my friend.

We have lots of friends in our class.

God plans for us to have friends.

Thank you, God, for friends.

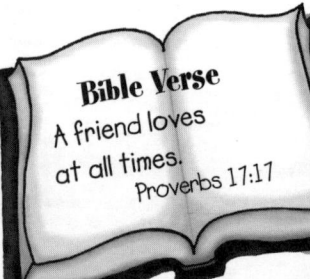

Bible Verse
A friend loves at all times.
Proverbs 17:17

Have the children stand in a circle. Tell the children the story. Have the children repeat the refrain and do the motions each time the refrain appears in the story.

The Story

David lived with King Saul. He became friends with King Saul's son, Jonathan.

**David and Jonathan were very good friends.
Stomp, stomp, clap, clap,** (*Stomp twice; clap twice.*)
Stretch and bend. (*Stretch arms over head; bend over.*)

One day Jonathan wanted to give David a special gift. He gave David his robe and his belt.

**David and Jonathan were very good friends.
Stomp, stomp, clap, clap,** (*Stomp twice; clap twice.*)
Stretch and bend. (*Stretch arms over head; bend over.*)

David knew the robe and belt were special to Jonathan. He was happy to have Jonathan's gift. David put on the robe and belt.

**David and Jonathan were very good friends.
Stomp, stomp, clap, clap,** (*Stomp twice; clap twice.*)
Stretch and bend. (*Stretch arms over head; bend over.*)

David and Jonathan made a promise to each other. They promised that they would always be very good friends.

**David and Jonathan were very good friends.
Stomp, stomp, clap, clap,** (*Stomp twice; clap twice.*)
Stretch and bend. (*Stretch arms over head; bend over.*)

David and Jonathan kept their promise to each other. They helped each other. They showed love to each other.

**David and Jonathan were very good friends.
Stomp, stomp, clap, clap,** (*Stomp twice; clap twice.*)
Stretch and bend. (*Stretch arms over head; bend over.*)

(Based on 1 Samuel 18:1-4.)

© 1998 Abingdon Press.

Special Friends

David had a special friend,
Jonathan was his name.
They liked to be together,
To laugh and sing and play.

We have many special friends,
Just listen to their names.
There's (*name each child in your class*).
We laugh and sing and play.

(Based on 1 Samuel 18:1-4.)

© 1990 Graded Press.

Queen Esther, Queen Esther

by Daphna Flegal

According to Jewish tradition the story of Esther is told as a melodrama. Tell the children that you want them to help you tell today's Bible story. Explain that the story is about a very brave woman named Esther. Esther helped her people. **Say: Each time I say the name Esther, I want you to say, "Yea!"** *Then explain that the story also has a bad man named Haman.* **Say: Each time I say the name Haman, I want you to say, "Boo!"** *(Remind the children that it can be fun to boo the bad guy in the story, but it is unkind to boo people.)*

The Story

Esther was very beautiful. She was also kind and loving. She lived with her cousin. **Esther** and her cousin were Jews. They loved God.

One day the king decided to marry a new queen. **Esther** went with her cousin to the palace to meet the king. When the king met **Esther**, he chose her to be his new queen. She was very happy. **Esther** liked being the queen and living in the palace.

Haman worked for the king. He was a selfish man. **Haman** thought he was more important than other people. **Haman** did not like the Jews. He wanted to do something to hurt the Jews. **Haman** tricked the king into making a law to kill all people who were Jews.

Queen **Esther** and her cousin were very upset. They were Jewish. "You must help our people," her cousin told Queen **Esther**. "You must talk to the king."

"I'm afraid," said Queen **Esther**. "The king might decide to kill me."

"You must be brave," said her cousin.

Queen **Esther** decided she would be brave. She asked her people to pray for her. **Esther** knew that God wanted her to help her people. She went to the king. **Esther** told him that she was a Jew. Queen **Esther** told the king about **Haman's** plan to kill all the Jews.

The king was very angry. He loved Queen **Esther**. He did not want the Jews killed. The king ordered his men to take **Haman** away. Queen **Esther** helped her people.

(Based on Esther 2–8.)

© 1997 Abingdon Press.

Teacher Talk

The Bible tells the story of Queen Esther.

We can help others.

Esther helped her people.

You are important to God.

Bible Verse
They held a joyful holiday with feasting and happiness.
Esther 8:17, Good News Bible, adapted

God Is Good
by Susan Isbell

Teacher Talk

God has created a wonderful world.

God has created you.

You are a wonderful creation.

Have the children do the motions suggested in the story.

The Story

Response:
God is good.
(*Extend both arms toward the front.*)
God is great.
(*Open both arms to the sides.*)
Let's praise God
(*Raise both arms over your head.*)
And celebrate!
(*Clap three times.*)

The light, the dark,
The night, the day,
God created in a special way.
(*Response*)

The earth, the sky,
The moon, the sun,
God created every one.
(*Response*)

The birds, the fish,
The plants, the trees,
God created each of these.
(*Response*)

Animals so big,
Animals so small,
God created one and all.
(*Response*)

Man and woman,
Boy and girl,
God created all the world.
(*Response*)

(Based on Psalm 8; Genesis 1:1-31.)

© 1997 Cokesbury.

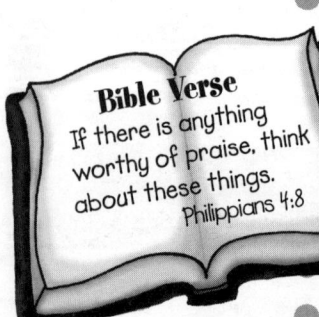

Bible Verse
If there is anything worthy of praise, think about these things.
Philippians 4:8

The Book of Psalms
by Susan Isbell

Psalms is a book of Bible songs.
(*Hold hands like a book.*)
Listen and you will know
(*Cup hand to ear.*)
How Bible people gave thanks and praise
(*Make praying hands.*)
To God so long ago.
(*Hold arms upward.*)

(Based on the Book of Psalms.)

© 1997 Cokesbury.

Wonderful Things

by Daphna Flegal

Have the children say the phrase, "Praise God! Tell of the wonderful things God has done," each time it appears in the story.

The Story

In the beginning God created the heavens and the earth.

Response:
Praise God! Tell of the wonderful things God has done. (*Cup hands around mouth.*)

God created day and night.
(*Response*)

God created sky, earth, and water.
(*Response*)

God created all kinds of plants.
(*Response*)

God created fish and water creatures.
(*Response*)

God created birds and flying creatures.
(*Response*)

God created all kinds of animals.
(*Response*)

God created people.
(*Response*)

God's creation is good.
(*Response*)

(Based on Psalm 9:1; Genesis 1:1-31.)

© 1996 Cokesbury.

Clap Your Praise
by Susan Isbell

(*Clap hands.*)
Clap, clap, clap your praise,
Clap your praise to God.
Praise God!

(*Shake hands.*)
Shake, shake, shake your praise,
Shake your praise to God.
Praise God!

(*Stomp feet.*)
Stomp, stomp, stomp your praise,
Stomp your praise to God.
Praise God!

(*Put first finger to lips and whisper.*)
Whisper, whisper, whisper your praise,
Whisper your praise to God.
Praise God!

(Based on Psalm 9:1.)

© 1994 Cokesbury.

Teacher Talk

God has made a wonderful world.

Thank you, God, for everything you have made.

Let's explore!

Bible Verse
I will tell of all the wonderful things God has done.
Psalm 9:1, Good News Bible, adapted

Come, Little Sheep

by Daphna Flegal

Teacher Talk

The Bible tells the story of David, the shepherd boy.

David trusted God.

We can trust God to take care of us.

Sheep

Materials needed: glue, tape, bandanna, cotton balls

Photocopy the sheep for each child (see page 46). Give each child a sheep. Let the children decorate the sheep by gluing cotton balls onto the sheep. Fold each sheep along the dotted lines. Glue or tape the sides of the sheep together, leaving the bottom open. Show the children how to put their hands inside the bottom opening of the sheep to make hand puppets.

Say: Our Bible story today is about David. Let's pretend that I am David.

Tie a bandanna around your head like a shepherd's headband.

Say: Let's pretend that you are all my sheep. Each time I say, "Come, little sheep," I want you to hold up your sheep puppets and say, "Baa, baa, baa."

The Story

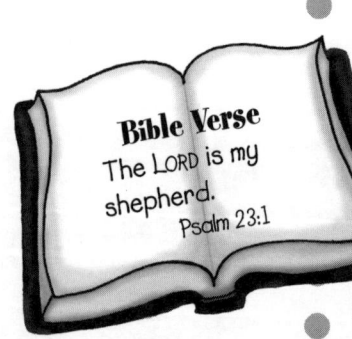

Bible Verse
The LORD is my shepherd.
Psalm 23:1

My name is David. I'm a shepherd. I take care of my family's sheep. My sheep follow me wherever I lead them. They know the sound of my voice. **Come, little sheep.**

Baa, baa, baa.

My sheep follow me to find green grass to eat. **Come, little sheep.**

Baa, baa, baa.

My sheep follow me to find cool water to drink. **Come, little sheep.**

Baa, baa, baa.

Sometimes one sheep will get lost. I look and look until I find the lost sheep. **Come, little sheep.**

Baa, baa, baa.

O Taste and See

by Daphna Flegal

Materials needed: one or more of the foods mentioned in the poem (blueberry muffins, caramel, lemon drops, animal crackers, popcorn, strawberry ice cream, carrots, bananas, green grapes), napkins

Give each child a snack of one of the foods mentioned in the poem. Say the poem as the children are eating. Be aware of any children with food allergies. Choose a food that everyone can eat.

Have the children echo the phrase, "O taste and see that the Lord is good!" whenever it appears in the poem.

The Story

Juicy red apples, thick chocolate cake,
Blueberry muffins ready to bake.
O taste and see that the Lord is good!

Sticky, sweet caramel; a sour lemon drop;
Animal crackers; corn that you pop.
O taste and see that the Lord is good!

Strawberry ice cream, carrots that crunch,
Yellow bananas, green grapes in a bunch.
O taste and see that the Lord is good!

(Based on Psalm 34:8.)

© 1990 Graded Press.

Teacher Talk

We thank God for good things to eat.

What's your favorite food to eat?

Thank you, God, for our senses.

God plans for our tongues to taste.

How does this taste?

Bible Verse
O taste and see that the LORD is good.
Psalm 34:8

Worship the Lord With Joy

by Daphna Flegal

Teacher Talk

What a joyful noise.

I feel like dancing with joy.

I hear lots of joyful noise.

Thank you, God, for the feeling called joy.

Bible Verse
Make a joyful noise to the LORD, all the earth.
Psalm 100:1

Have the children do the motions as indicated in the story. When you say the phrases in bold, pause after each sentence and have the children repeat it.

The Story

Make happy sounds to God,
Clap, clap, clap!
(*Clap hands.*)
Make happy sounds to God,
Tap, tap, tap!
(*Tap toes.*)
Make happy sounds to God,
Snap, snap, snap!
(*Tap fingers together.*)
Worship the Lord with joy
And sing happy, happy songs!

God made us.
We belong to God.

Make happy sounds to God,
Clap, clap, clap!
(*Clap hands.*)
Make happy sounds to God,
Tap, tap, tap!
(*Tap toes.*)
Make happy sounds to God,
Snap, snap, snap!
(*Tap fingers together.*)
Worship the Lord with joy
And sing happy, happy songs!

Give thanks to God;
Give praise to God.

Make happy sounds to God,
Clap, clap, clap!
(*Clap hands.*)
Make happy sounds to God,
Tap, tap, tap!
(*Tap toes.*)
Make happy sounds to God,
Snap, snap, snap!
(*Tap fingers together.*)
Worship the Lord with joy
And sing happy, happy songs!

God is good;
God loves us forever.

Make happy sounds to God,
Clap, clap, clap!
(*Clap hands.*)
Make happy sounds to God,
Tap, tap, tap!
(*Tap toes.*)
Make happy sounds to God,
Snap, snap, snap!
(*Tap fingers together.*)
Worship the Lord with joy
And sing happy, happy songs!

(Based on Psalm 100.)

© 1995 Cokesbury.

Sing a New Song

by Sharilyn S. Adair

Give each child a tambourine or see the instructions on page 50 for the children to make their own tambourines.

The Story

Response:
Praise the Lord!
Let us praise the Lord!
How shall we praise?
What are the ways?

One way is learning a new song to sing.
Voices for singing are wonderful things.

(Response)

One way is dancing; let's dance as we sing.
Feet made for dancing are wonderful things.

(Response)

One way is shaking our loud tambourines.
Drums that make music are wonderful things.

(Response)

Singing and dancing and playing are ways
We thank God, who made us, and that's how we praise.

Praise the Lord!

(Based on Psalm 149.)

© 2000 Abingdon Press.

Sing Praise to God
by Sharilyn S. Adair

Sing the following stanza to the tune of "Hot Cross Buns." Let the children dance in a circle as you sing.

Praise the Lord.
Praise the Lord.
We are happy, oh so happy.
Praise the Lord.

(Based on Psalm 149.)

Teacher Talk

How does music make you feel?

Show me how you can dance to music.

We can praise God with music.

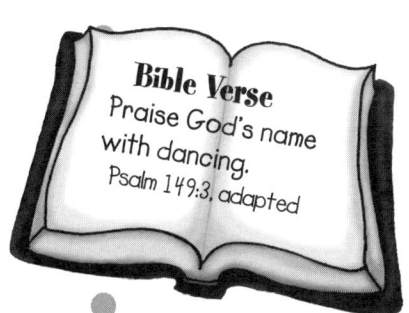

Bible Verse
Praise God's name with dancing.
Psalm 149:3, adapted

Praise the Lord!

by Sharilyn S. Adair

Teacher Talk

How does music make you feel?

Show me how you can move your body to the music.

We can praise God with our bodies.

Bible Verse
Praise God with drums and dancing.
Psalm 150:4, Good News Bible, adapted

Tambourine

Materials needed: curling ribbon; crayons or markers; glue; shallow containers; paper plates; construction paper; paper punch; yarn or chenille stems; noisemakers such as jingle bells, pop-top rings from soft drink cans, metal soft drink bottle caps and hammer and nail, or paper clips

Give each child a copy of the picture of the woman dancing and playing a tambourine (see page 52) and short pieces of curling ribbon. Invite the children to color their pictures of the woman. Let the children decorate their pictures with short pieces of curling ribbon. Pour glue into shallow containers. Show the children how to stick one end of the pieces of curling ribbon into the glue to make streamers for the tambourines. Put the pictures aside to dry.

For each child you will need six small sources of a jingling or clanging sound. Small to medium-sized jingle bells work best; but if you do not have them, make substitutes. Place two pop-top rings from soft drink cans on a loop of yarn or a looped section of chenille stem; or make holes in the middle of two metal soft drink bottle caps with a hammer and nail, place the caps back to back, and thread the yarn or chenille stem through the caps. Three paper clips can also be strung on a loop of yarn or chenille stem, but they don't make quite as much sound as the other items. Tie the yarn or twist the chenille stems to make a loop about one inch in diameter.

Give each child a paper plate and invite the children to decorate the plates by gluing on scraps of construction paper. Use a paper punch to punch six holes around the rim of each child's plate. Help the children attach jingle bells, pop-top rings, bottle caps, or paper clips to their tambourines by threading yarn or sections of chenille stem through the noisemakers and then through the holes and tying the yarn or twisting the chenille stem. Thread lengths of curling ribbon through the holes and tie them to the plates to form two streamers at each hole. Offer ribbon in more than one color and let the children choose the colors of their streamers.

The Story

Praise the LORD! (*Shake tambourines.*)

Praise God in his sanctuary;
   praise him in his mighty firmament!

Praise the LORD! (*Shake tambourines.*)
Praise him for his mighty deeds;
   praise him according to his
   surpassing greatness!

Praise the LORD! (*Shake tambourines.*)

Praise him with trumpet sound;
   praise him with lute and harp!

Praise the LORD! (*Shake tambourines.*)

Praise him with tambourine and
   dance;
   praise him with strings and
   pipe!

Praise the LORD! (*Shake tambourines.*)

Praise him with clanging
   cymbals;
   praise him with loud
   clashing cymbals!

Praise the LORD! (*Shake tambourines.*)

Let everything that breathes
   praise the LORD! (*Shake tambourines.*)

Praise the LORD! (*Shake tambourines.*)

(Based on Psalm 150.)

© 2000 Abingdon Press.

Praise God!
by Daphna Flegal

Praise God!
Praise God at church;
Praise God in all the world!
Praise God for all the mighty things
   God has done;
Praise God because God is great!
Praise God with trumpets;
Praise God with harps!
Praise God with tambourines;
Praise God with dance;
Praise God with lutes;
Praise God with loud crashing
   cymbals!
Let everyone praise God!
Praise God!

(Based on Psalm 150.)

© 1995 Cokesbury.

Be a Friend
by Susan Isbell

Have the children shout, "Be a friend!" after you say the Bible verse each time.

The Story

Good morning, boys and girls! (*Wave to the children. Let the children wave back.*) It's great to see all of you.

I'm going to tell you about some books that are part of a special book. That special book is called the Bible. The Bible is made up of many books, and today I am going to tell you about one of those books called Proverbs. Can you say, "Proverbs"? (*Give the children time to repeat the word.*)

Proverbs is a collection of wise sayings. Long ago some very wise men wrote down good ideas that they thought would help people live better lives. They put them together in a book in the Bible.

One of the proverbs is about being a friend. I've got a poem about being a friend. Can you help me say it?

A friend is a person you really enjoy.
A friend can be a girl.
A friend can be a boy.

Response:
A friend loves at all times.
(*shout*) Be a friend!
A friend loves at all times.
(*shout*) Be a friend!

A friend is a person who's lots of fun.
Friends can come in groups,
Or maybe just one.
(*Response*)

A friend can make you laugh.
A friend can make you cry.
But a real friend gives love and care a try.
(*Response*)

(Based on Proverbs 17:17.)

© 1997 Cokesbury.

Teacher Talk

A friend is a gift from God.

You and your friends are important to God.

I'm glad you're my friend.

We have lots of friends in our class.

God plans for us to have friends.

Thank you, God, for friends.

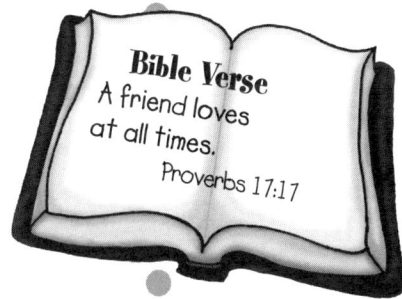

Bible Verse
A friend loves at all times.
Proverbs 17:17

For Everything There Is a Season

by Sharilyn S. Adair

Teacher Talk

God plans for the seasons.

The winter season follows fall.

The spring season follows winter.

The summer season follows spring.

The fall season follows summer.

We thank God for the seasons.

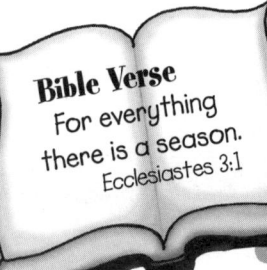

Bible Verse
For everything there is a season.
Ecclesiastes 3:1

Have the children stand. Say: Today's Bible story is about God's plan for seasons and about how we can see changes in God's world from one season to the next. As you listen to the story poem, watch me and do as I do. Encourage the children to do the refrain after each verse.

The Story

For everything there is a season:
(*Hold arms out from sides; turn around.*)
Winter, spring, summer, fall.
(*Hold up four fingers, one at a time.*)
For everything there is a season.
(*Hold arms out from sides; turn around.*)
We thank God for them all.
(*Fold hands in prayer.*)

God plans a time just right to plant
The seed for grass to grow.
(*Pretend to plant a seed in the ground.*)
God plans that when the grass gets tall,
The time is right to mow.
(*Hold both hands in front of you as though pushing a mower and say "Rrrrrrr."*)
And then God turns the green grass brown
And covers it with snow.
(*Make a whooshing sound.*)

For everything there is a season:
(*Hold arms out from sides; turn around.*)
Winter, spring, summer, fall.
(*Hold up four fingers, one at a time.*)
For everything there is a season.
(*Hold arms out from sides; turn around.*)
We thank God for them all.
(*Fold hands in prayer.*)

God plans for springtime rain and flowers;
(*Hold hands above head and wiggle fingers as you lower them to waist level.*)
God plans for summer sun;
(*Make a circle above your head.*)
God plans for fall and tumbling leaves,
(*Wave your arms back and forth like leaves blowing in the wind.*)
For snow and winter fun.
(*Hug arms around body as if cold.*)
God plans for spring to come again
When wintertime is done.
(*Make a circle above your head.*)

For everything there is a season:
(*Hold arms out from sides; turn around.*)
Winter, spring, summer, fall.
(*Hold up four fingers, one at a time.*)
For everything there is a season.
(*Hold arms out from sides; turn around.*)
We thank God for them all.
(*Fold hands in prayer.*)

(Based on Ecclesiastes 3:1.)

© 1999 Abingdon Press.

The Seasons
by Bettye Saunders

God made winter, spring, summer, and fall.
They are called the seasons.
Each is different; each is good.
God made them for a reason.

There's a time to plant seeds for flowers and food,
A time when a cold swim is nice.
There's a time for pumpkins and Thanksgiving,
A time for snow and ice.

We are thankful for the seasons.
God made them all.
Each is very special,
Winter, spring, summer, and fall.

(Based on Ecclesiastes 3:1; Genesis 8:22.)

© 1996 Cokesbury.

An Echo Fish Story

by Daphna Flegal

Teacher Talk

The Bible tells the story of Jonah and a big fish.

We can pray to God any time.

God hears our prayers.

Jonah prayed to God.

The Story

"Jonah, Jonah," said God one day, (*Shake pointer finger.*)
"Go to Ninevah, go right away!" (*Point far away.*)

"No, no, no," Jonah answered that day, (*Put hands on legs.*)
"I won't go to Ninevah. I'll run away." (*Run in place.*)

So Jonah took a ride on a great big boat, (*Rock back and forth.*)
And went to sleep while he was afloat. (*Place hands under cheek as if sleeping.*)

Then the wind started blowing, and the waves crashed about. (*Rock back and forth.*)
"Wake up, Jonah," the men began to shout. (*Cup hands around mouth.*)

Jonah woke up and saw the ocean waves. (*Put hand over eyes.*)
"Throw me in the water so that you can be saved." (*Pretend to dive in water.*)

The men picked Jonah up and threw him in the sea. (*Pretend to swim.*)
Where a great big fish just happened to be. (*Put palms together to make fish with hands.*)

The fish swallowed Jonah down into its belly. (*Rub stomach.*)
He stayed there three days, all wet and smelly. (*Pinch nose.*)

While inside the fish, Jonah prayed and prayed. (*Fold hands in prayer.*)
God heard his prayers from where they were made. (*Cup hands around ears.*)

The fish spit Jonah out onto dry land. (*Make fish with hands; open palms and then snap them back together.*)
Then Jonah went to Ninevah, just as God planned. (*Walk in place.*)

(Based on Jonah 1-2.)

© 1997 Abingdon Press.

Bible Verse
Pray at all times.
Romans 12:12.
Good News Bible

New Testament

Goals:

1. The children will be introduced to Jesus, God's Son.

2. The children will hear stories about Jesus' life and ministry.

3. The children will begin to understand that Jesus grew from a baby to a boy to a man.

4. The children will learn that Jesus showed God's love to all people.

5. The children will discover that Jesus loves each one of them.

6. The children will hear stories about people who loved and followed Jesus.

Use these stories to introduce your children to Jesus, God's Son. Teach them that Jesus showed us God's love and that Jesus loves each one of us. Help them connect the stories of Jesus as a baby to the stories of Jesus as a man. Above all, use these stories as opportunities to remind your children that Jesus loves us all.

Introduce your children to some of the Bible people who became followers of Jesus. These stories remind us of how we can live as followers of Jesus.

Twinkle, Twinkle

by Lorri Coates and Barbara McKone

Teacher Talk

People all over the world celebrate Christmas.

Stars and light are a special part of the Christmas story.

God loves everyone in the world.

Starscope

Materials needed: crayons or markers, tape, white paper or construction paper, glitter or confetti, glue, yarn, paper punch

Photocopy the starscope page (see page 60) for each child. Let the children decorate the stars with crayons or markers. Help each child roll the starscope page lengthwise into a tube. Tape the edges together. Show each child how to hold the starscope up to one eye to pretend to look at the stars.

Draw a simple star on a piece of white paper or construction paper. Make it as big as the paper will allow. Decorate the star with glitter or confetti. Use a paper punch to punch a hole in the top of the star. Thread a piece of yarn through the hole and tie it in a knot. Hang or mount the star in your story area. Have the children bring their starscopes and stand in an area of the room opposite the star. Lead the children around the room to the star as you tell the story and do the suggested motions.

The Story

Let's pretend that we're the wise men who followed a bright star to find a new king. Everyone, get out your starscope! (*Have the children look through their starscopes.*) Look through your starscopes at the stars. See the three stars in a line. (*Point overhead.*) Look! (*Turn your starscope so that it is facing the star in your story area.*) There's one that's brighter and larger than all of the others.

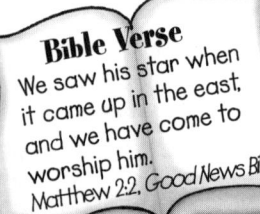

Bible Verse
We saw his star when it came up in the east, and we have come to worship him.
Matthew 2:2, *Good News Bible*

The bright star tells us that a special king has been born. We must go to find this king and bring him gifts. What shall we give him? (*Encourage the children to make suggestions.*) Put your gift in your bag and hold on to your starscope. Everyone, up on your camel. Let's go! (*Pretend to place something in a bag and then get on a camel.*) Let's sing a traveling song to make the trip go faster. (*Pretend to ride a camel as you sing the words printed at right to the tune of "Twinkle, Twinkle, Little Star." Lead the children around the room.*)

Twinkle, twinkle, shining star,
We are wise men from afar,
Following a star so bright,
Looking for a king this night.
Twinkle, twinkle, shining star,
We are wise men from afar.

Stop and look through your starscope. (*Look through starscopes.*) See the star? It's leading us to a little town called Bethlehem. I'm getting excited, aren't you? Let's head for Bethlehem. (*Pretend to ride camels.*) Let's sing our traveling song as we go. (*Sing the words printed below to the tune of "Twinkle, Twinkle, Little Star" as you lead the children to your story area.*)

> ### Look!
> by Susan Isbell
>
> Look! A star shining bright.
> Look! A star lights up the night.
> "Look! A star!" said wise men three.
> "Follow that star to where Jesus will be."
>
> (Based on Matthew 2:1-12.)
>
> © 1996 Cokesbury.

Twinkle, twinkle, shining star,
We are wise men from afar,
Following a star so bright,
Looking for a king this night.
Twinkle, twinkle, shining star,
We are wise men from afar.

Quick! Get out your starscopes. (*Look through starscopes.*) There it is, just up that hill! A house with the star overhead! That's where we will find the new king. We're here! Tie up your camel. Open your bag and get out your gift. Everyone, knock on the door of the house. (*Pretend to knock.*) Look! The new king is Jesus! Let's lay our gifts before Jesus. (*Encourage the children to kneel and to pretend to place their gifts underneath the star.*) What a wonderful gift God has given us!

(Based on Matthew 2:1-12.)

© 1998 Abingdon Press.

60 Permission granted to photocopy. © 1998 Abingdon Press.

Happy Teachings

by Daphna Flegal

Happy Stick

Materials needed: scissors; crayons or markers; paper plate; cardboard tube, ruler, or paint stirrer; glue or tape

Photocopy and cut out one copy of the happy face (see page 62). Let the children decorate the happy face. Glue the happy face onto a paper plate. Glue or tape a cardboard tube, ruler, or paint stirrer (usually obtained free from paint stores or paint departments at discount stores) to the back of the paper plate to make a handle. **Say: I want you to help me tell the story today. I will give you the happy stick to hold when it is your turn to talk.**

The Story

Let's think about being happy. When are you happy? Are you happy when your mother gives you a hug? Are you happy when you eat ice cream? Are you happy when you stay up past your bedtime? (*Child's name*), when are you happy? (*Give the happy stick to the child named. Let the child respond to your question. Give the stick to other children and let them respond to the question.*)

What do you do when you feel happy? Do you laugh? Do you smile? Do you jump up and down? (*Child's name*), what do you do when you feel happy? (*Give the happy stick to the child named. Let the child respond to your question. Give the stick to other children and let them respond to the question.*)

Do you have someone you like to be with when you feel happy? Is it your friend? your mom or dad? your brother or sister? (*Child's name*), who do you like to be with when you feel happy? (*Give the happy stick to the child named. Let the child respond to your question. Make sure every child has had a turn holding the stick and answering at least one question.*)

Jesus' friends wanted to be with Jesus. They were happy to listen to Jesus teach about God. One day Jesus sat down with his friends and said:

Happy are people who trust God. Happy are people when they are sad and God helps them feel better. Happy are people who do not think they are most important. Happy are people who do what God wants them to do. Happy are people who forgive others. Happy are people who love God. Happy are people who work for peace.

Be happy and glad!

(Based on Matthew 5:1-12.)

© 1998 Abingdon Press.

Teacher Talk

God loves you when you are happy.

God loves you when you are sad.

God loves you all the time.

You look happy!

Bible Verse
Be happy and glad.
Matthew 5:12,
Good News Bible

Talking to God

by Daphna Flegal

Prayer Square Face

Materials needed: scissors, glue, empty cereal box, paper

Photocopy and cut out one copy of the prayer square face (see page 65). Glue the square onto the front or back of an empty cereal box so that the opening of the cereal box is at the bottom of the prayer square face. Cut four two-inch-wide strips of paper. Accordion-fold each strip. Glue one strip on each side of the box to represent arms. Glue two strips at the bottom of the box to represent legs. Show the children the prayer square. Cut paper into one-inch-wide strips. Let the children add hair to the square by gluing on the paper strips.

Show the children the prayer square puppet. Use the puppet to tell the Bible story.

The Story

My name is Prayer Square. I like to pray. That means I like to talk to God. In the morning when I first wake up, I pray, "Thank you, God, for this sunny day." Or maybe I pray, "Thank you, God, for this rainy day."

Sometimes I talk to God about how I feel. I pray, "I feel happy today. Thank you, God, for happy feelings." Or I pray, "I don't feel good today. Help me feel better soon."

When I eat my breakfast, I pray, "Thank you, God, for cereal and milk." What do you like to eat for breakfast? (*Encourage the children to respond.*) Then you can pray, "Thank you, God, for (*name the things the children named*)."

After breakfast I play with my friends. I pray, "Thank you, God, for friends." You are all my friends. "Thank you, God, for (*name each child*)."

At lunchtime my friends and I sing a prayer. (*Sing the prayer below to the tune of "London Bridge."*)

Thank you, God, for food to eat,
Food to eat, food to eat.
Thank you, God, for food to eat.
Amen.

Teacher Talk

God will hear us when we pray.

Jesus taught his followers a special prayer.

God planned for everyone to have good food to eat.

We thank God for food.

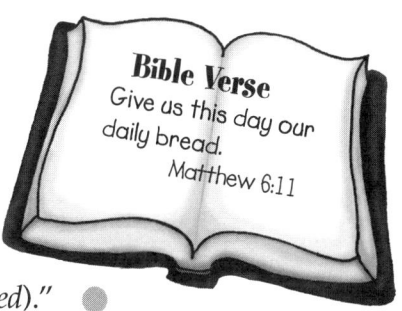

Bible Verse
Give us this day our daily bread.
Matthew 6:11

After lunch I like to listen to a story from the Bible. The Bible is a special book that tells us about God and Jesus. The Bible tells us that Jesus talked to God. He thanked God for food. Jesus asked God to help him make sick people well. And he asked God to help him do hard things.

Jesus' friends saw Jesus talking to God. The friends asked Jesus to teach them how to talk to God. They said, "Jesus, teach us to pray."

Jesus taught his friends a special prayer. We call the prayer the Lord's Prayer. Listen while I say the prayer for you.

(*Say this version of the Lord's Prayer, or repeat the version used by your church family.*)

Our Father in heaven,
    hallowed be your name,
    your kingdom come,
    your will be done, on earth
        as in heaven.
Give us today our daily bread.
Forgive us our sins
    as we forgive those who sin
        against us.
Save us from the time of trial
    and deliver us from evil.
For the kingdom, the power, and the glory
        are yours
    now and for ever. Amen.

English translation of The Lord's Prayer *by the International Consultation on English Texts. From* The United Methodist Hymnal, *894.*

(Based on Matthew 6:9-13.)

© 1998 Abingdon Press.

Amen, Amen, Amen

Have the children say, "Amen, amen, amen!" with you whenever it appears in the story.

God will hear us when we pray.
(Whisper) **Amen, amen, amen!**

In the night or in the day,
(Shout) **Amen, amen, amen!**

When we sing and when we play,
(Whisper) **Amen, amen, amen!**

God always hears us when we pray.
(Shout) **Amen, amen, amen!**

(Based on Matthew 6:9-13.)

© *1999 Cokesbury.*

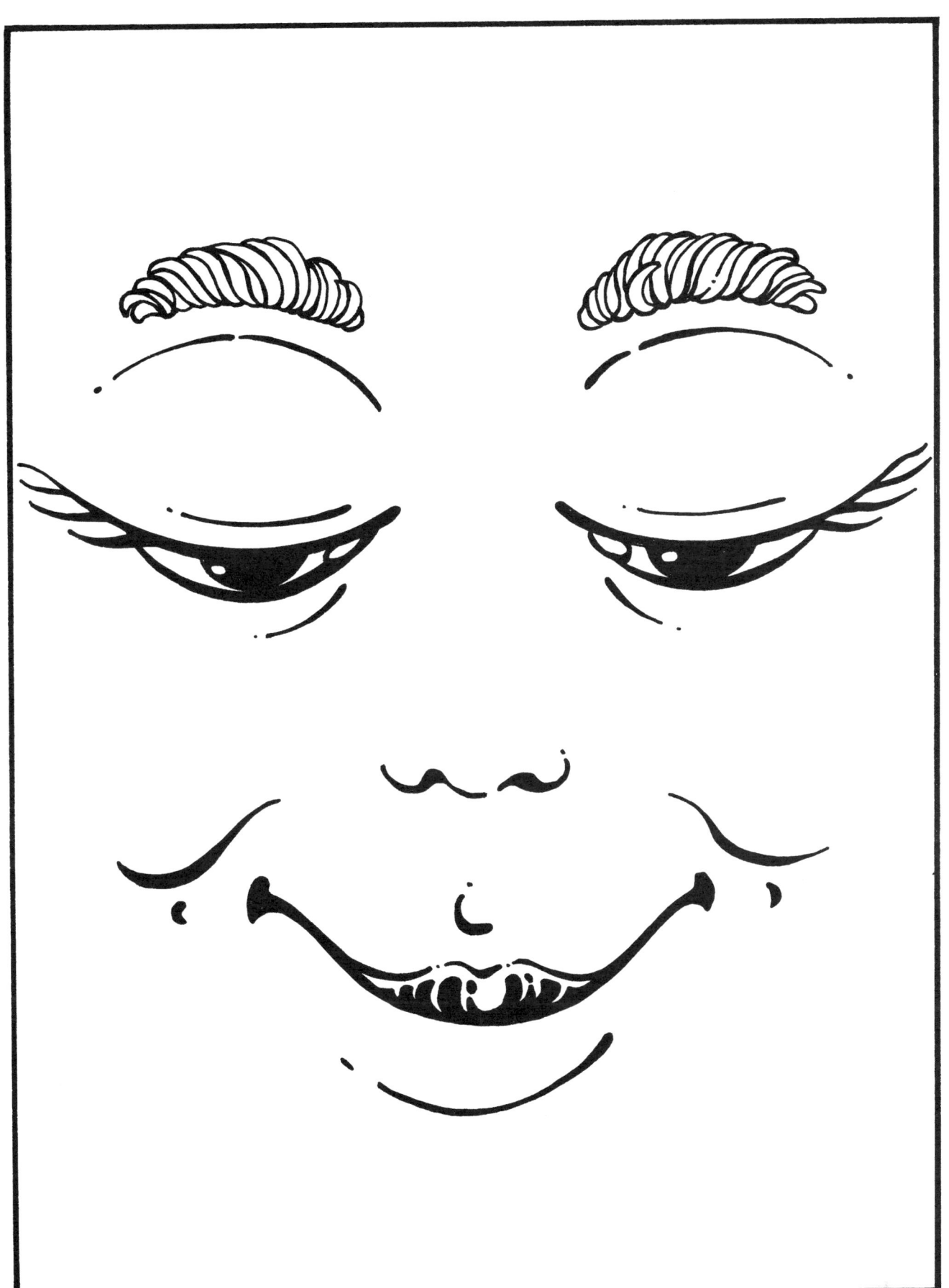

*Candi
10-5-03
(noone there)*

God Cares
by Susan Isbell

Teacher Talk

Each one of us is different.

Each one of us is special.

God loves each one of us.

You're very important to God.

God wants you to take care of yourself.

God loves you and cares about you.

The Story

One day Jesus was sitting on the hillside, telling stories of God's love to the people who came to listen. Jesus wanted the people to know that God loved every man, woman, boy, and girl and that God would take care of them.

Jesus saw the birds flying overhead in the sky.

"Look!" Jesus said. "See the birds in the sky? They look for food. God has planned for the birds to find food to eat."

The people on the hillside saw the birds pecking at the ground for food. The people knew that God cared about the birds.

Jesus reached down and touched a flower growing in the grass.

Let's Pretend
by Susan Isbell

Let's pretend we are birds flying all around.
(Flap arms and move in a circle.)

Let's pretend we are flowers growing in the ground.
(Crouch down and then slowly stretch up as if growing.)

Now let's be still and listen—sit very quietly—
(Sit down; put finger to lips and whisper.)

To a story of God's love for you and me!
(Point to the children; point to yourself.)

(Based on Matthew 6:25-34.)

© 1994 Cokesbury.

"See the beautiful flowers?" Jesus said. "They have bright, cheerful colors. God planned for the flowers and sends the rain and the sunshine to make them grow."

Bible Verse
God cares about you.
1 Peter 5:7, adapted

The people looked at the flowers. They knew that Jesus was right. God cared for the flowers.

"You are people," Jesus said. "You are special creations of God. If you know that God cares for birds and flowers, surely you know that God cares for people even more."

The people thought about what Jesus said. God planned for birds, for flowers, and for people. The people were thankful that God cared for them.

(Based on Matthew 6:25-34.)

© 1994 Cokesbury.

Jesus Heals Peter's Mother-in-law

by Sharilyn S. Adair

Hot 'n Happy Hats

Materials needed: scissors, crayons, tape

Photocopy and cut out the happy and sad strips (see page 68). Give each child a sad face strip. Let the children color the strips with crayons. Give each child a happy face strip. Let the children color the strips with crayons. Help each child tape the happy face strip to the sad face strip to make one strip. Measure the strip around each child's head. Make the hat a little loose so the child can turn the hat around on her or his head. Tape the ends together.

The Story

(*Have the children turn their hats so that the happy faces are in front.*) One day Peter's mother-in-law, the mother of Peter's wife, was doing some housework. She sang a song as she swept her floor. The house was dark and quiet, and a cool breeze blew in through one window.

It was such a nice breeze that the mother-in-law should have felt cool, but she didn't. She felt hot! "Oh dear!" she said. "I don't feel very well. I have a fever. I will lie down for a while." (*Have the children turn their hats so that the sad faces are in front.*)

Soon Peter came home. He brought his friend Jesus with him. "I'm glad that it is cool in our house," said Peter.

"Yes," said Jesus. "The cool breeze feels good." (*Have the children turn their hats so that the happy faces are in front.*)

Just then Peter saw his mother-in-law lying on a mat in the corner. "What's the matter?" he asked. "Do you feel sick?" Peter felt her forehead. It felt warm. "You have a fever," he said to her. (*Have the children turn their hats so that the sad faces are in front.*)

"Let me feel," said Jesus. Jesus touched her hand. Suddenly the fever went away! (*Have the children turn their hats so that the happy faces are in front.*)

"I feel fine now. Thank you, Jesus, for making my fever go away," she said. "Now let me get you some warm food and some cool water."

(Based on Matthew 8:14-15.)

© 1998 Abingdon Press.

Teacher Talk

God plans for people to help us stay healthy.

God plans for people to help us when we are sick.

God is with us when we are sick and when we are well.

God is always with us.

Bible Verse
Heal the sick.
Matthew 10:8,
Good News Bible

Little and Big

by Sharilyn S. Adair

Materials needed: small seed, such as a radish seed or poppy seed; large seed, such as a peach pit or lima bean

Teach the children the following signs for the concepts little and big. For little have them hold one thumb and forefinger close together but not touching. For big have them hold their arms far apart. Have the children practice the signs as you mention items that are little and big. Name contrasting items in pairs (baby, grownup; ant, elephant). **Say: Our story has little things and big things in it. Sometimes I will ask you to show me whether something in the story is little or big. When I ask you to show me a size, make one of the signs we just learned. Show me what you will do for a little thing.** *(Pause for responses.)* **Now show me what you will do for a big thing.** *(Pause for responses.)*

Begin by showing the children a small seed and a large seed.

The Story

These two things do not look alike, but they are the same kind of thing. What are they? *(Pause for answers.)* These are seeds. *(Hold up the small seed.)* Is this a little seed or a big seed? Show me. *(Pause for responses; then hold up the large seed.)* Is this a little seed or a big seed? Show me. *(Pause for responses.)*

Do you know what seeds do? *(Pause.)* Seeds grow into plants and sometimes even into trees. Trees are a special kind of plant. Are trees a little plant or a big plant? Show me. *(Pause.)*

One day Jesus was teaching. He told his followers about a mustard seed, which is a seed about this size. *(Hold up the small seed.)* What size is the mustard seed—little or big? Show me. *(Pause.)* Jesus said the little mustard seed might not look important. It is tiny. But guess what? This tiny little seed grows into a plant that is as big as a tree. Show me how big. *(Pause.)*

Jesus said that the plant that grows from the mustard seed is so big that it has branches for birds to build nests in. Could a bird build a nest in this tiny little seed? No, a bird could not fit even one of its feet on this tiny little seed. Show me how little. *(Pause.)* But without the tiny seed there would never be a big tree for the bird to make a nest in. Every mustard plant that is as big as a tree—show me how big *(pause)*—started out as a seed this small. Show me how little. *(Pause.)* This is an important little seed.

Jesus used the seed to teach his followers about what God is doing in the world. We can't see God, so we might think that God is not doing anything important. But God is doing wonderful things, just as the tiny seed—show me how little *(pause)*—grows into a great big tree. Show me how big. *(Pause.)*

(Based on Matthew 13:31-32.)

© 2000 Abingdon Press.

Teacher Talk

God made seeds.

Plants grow from seeds.

We can plant seeds and help them grow.

There are some seeds that we eat.

We thank God for seeds.

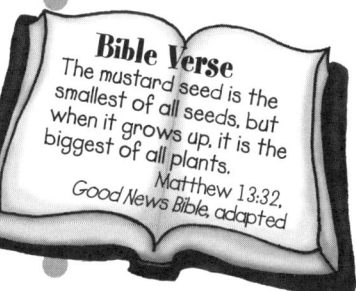

Bible Verse
The mustard seed is the smallest of all seeds, but when it grows up, it is the biggest of all plants.
Matthew 13:32,
Good News Bible, adapted

The Big, Big Windstorm

by Sharilyn S. Adair

Teacher Talk

There are many different ways to travel.

One way to travel on water is by boat.

Some boats have sails.

The Bible tells us a story about Jesus and his friends.

God is with us wherever we go.

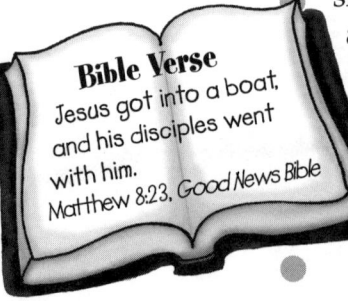

Bible Verse
Jesus got into a boat, and his disciples went with him.
Matthew 8:23, Good News Bible

Invite the children to copy your actions and to help provide sound effects as you tell the following story.

The Story

One day Jesus and his disciples were standing on the shore of a lake. Jesus had been teaching all day, and there were lots and lots of people around him and his disciples. Can you sound like a noisy crowd of people? (*Say, "Bzz! Bzz! Bzz!" and have the children repeat the sound several times.*)

Jesus said to the disciples, "There are too many people here. Let's get into our boat and go to the other side of the lake." So they got into a boat, and the disciples began to row the boat out into the lake. Let's row boats. (*Make fists with both hands, holding them out in front of you, palms down. Move them back to your sides as you bend your elbows. Repeat the action several times as the children copy you.*)

Jesus was sleepy. He found a pillow to lie down on. Soon he was fast asleep. What do you suppose he sounded like when he was asleep? (*Place your palms together and rest one cheek on them. Make snoring noises. Expect the children to giggle as they try to copy your sounds.*)

Soon the boat was far enough out into the lake for the sail to be put up. A small wind began blowing into the sail and gently pushing the boat along. (*Make a whishing sound by blowing gently as you whisper the word whish.*) Let's be boats moving over the water as the wind pushes us along. (*Have the children follow you in gliding steps around the story area as you continue to make the whishing sound. Return to your original place.*)

Jesus was still sleeping soundly near the front of the boat. (*Repeat the sleeping motion and snoring noises.*)

Oh dear! The little wind became a bigger wind. Soon it was a big, big wind. What do you think a big wind would sound like? (*Raise your arms and wave them back and forth as you say, "Whoosh! Whoosh! Whoosh!"*) The boat began to tumble back and forth in the water as the big wind pushed it around. Let's be boats being pushed around by a big wind. (*Have the children follow you as you take a series of three short forward steps first to one side and then to the other, swaying your body in the direction you are moving. Travel quickly around your story area in this manner as you say, "Whoosh! Whoosh! Whoosh." Return to your original place.)*

Water began pouring into the boat. What sound does moving water make? (*Say, "Splash! Splash! Splash!" and have the children repeat the words with you several times.*) But Jesus was still sound asleep. (*Repeat the sleeping motion and snoring noises.*)

Let's make all the noises that were going on right then. (*Have the children wave their arms and say, "Whoosh! Whoosh! Whoosh!" Then have them say, "Splash! Splash! Splash!" And finally have them make snoring noises.*) Oh my! It was a noisy time. The little boat with Jesus and the disciples in it was caught in a big, big windstorm.

The disciples were afraid. They ran to Jesus. "Wake up! Wake up!" they cried. "Save us from this terrible storm!"

Jesus woke up and stretched. Let's pretend we are waking up. (*Have the children stretch their hands above their heads.*) "Why are you afraid?" asked Jesus.

Then Jesus said to the big, big wind, "Peace. Be still." Suddenly the wind stopped blowing the boat around. Everything was very, very quiet. (*Hold your finger to your lips to hush the children. Let there be silence for about ten seconds.*)

The disciples were surprised and happy as the little boat rocked gently in the calm, quiet lake. Jesus had kept them safe from the big, big windstorm.

(Based on Matthew 8:23-26.)

© 2000 Abingdon Press.

Count and Chant

by Daphna Flegal

Teacher Talk

We use numbers every day for many things.

We can learn lots of new things.

God provides for all of our needs.

Fish Pictures

Materials needed: scissors, tape

Tape two of the small fish pictures (see page 73) on two of each child's fingers. Tape the five bread pictures on one of your hands. Say the poem below. Hold up the five bread pictures on your hand when you say, "Five loaves of bread." Have the children hold up their fingers with the fish pictures when you say, "and two little fish."

The Story

Five loaves of bread
(*Hold up five fingers.*)
And two little fish.
(*Hold up two fingers.*)
My, oh my, what a tasty dish!
(*Rub stomach.*)

Five thousand people came from far and near,
To see the man Jesus, God's Son so dear.
They sat on the hillside and listened all day
To the wonderful things Jesus had to say.

Five loaves of bread
(*Hold up five fingers.*)
And two little fish.
(*Hold up two fingers.*)
My, oh my, what a tasty dish!
(*Rub stomach.*)

They sat so long, it began to grow dark.
They became so hungry, they would eat a shark.
But when Jesus' friends took a look around,
A small boy's lunch was the food they found.

Five loaves of bread
(*Hold up five fingers.*)
And two little fish.

Bible Verse
There is a boy here who has five barley loaves and two fish.
John 6:9

(*Hold up two fingers.*)
My, oh my, what a tasty dish!
(*Rub stomach.*)

The boy was happy to share his lunch,
Though he didn't think it would feed this bunch.
But Jesus took the food and then calmly said,
"Thank you, God, for this fish and bread."

Five loaves of bread
(*Hold up five fingers.*)
And two little fish.
(*Hold up two fingers.*)
My, oh my, what a tasty dish!
(*Rub stomach.*)

Five loaves and two fish fed everyone there,
And they ate and they ate without a care.
They gathered the leftovers—twelve baskets when done.
They knew Jesus loved them, each and every one.

Five loaves of bread
(*Hold up five fingers.*)
And two little fish.
(*Hold up two fingers.*)
My, oh my, what a tasty dish!
(*Rub stomach.*)

(Based on John 6:1-14.)

© 1997 Abingdon Press.

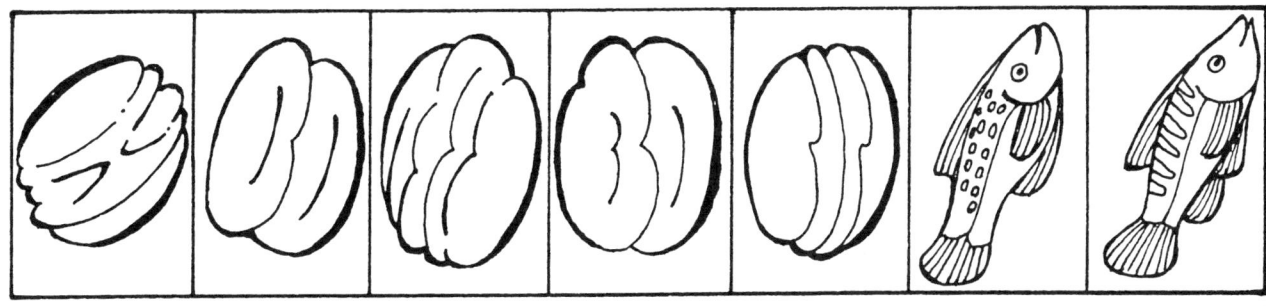

Three Servants

by Daphna Flegal

Teacher Talk

God gives each person talents to do special things.

God wants us to do good things with our talents.

Thank you, God, for our special talents.

Bible Verse
You have been trustworthy in a few things. I will put you in charge of many things. Matthew 25:21

Encourage the children to hold up fingers each time you name the servants in the story. Have each child to hold up one finger for Servant One, two fingers for Servant Two, and three fingers for Servant Three.

The Story

Once there was a rich man. He had three servants.

Servant One, Servant One,
Count on him to get things done.
Servant Two, Servant Two,
This man knew just what to do.
Servant Three, Servant Three,
He was lazy, you will see.

The rich man had to take a trip. He gave each of his servants money to use while he was gone.

Servant One, Servant One,
Count on him to get things done.
Servant Two, Servant Two,
This man knew just what to do.
Servant Three, Servant Three,
He was lazy, you will see.

Servant One used the money to do good things. Servant One had the BIGGEST bag of money. Servant Two used the money to do good things. Servant two had a BIG bag of money. But Servant Three used the money to do nothing. He had the SMALLEST bag of money. Then the master came home.

Servant One, Servant One,
Count on him to get things done.
Servant Two, Servant Two,
This man knew just what to do.
Servant Three, Servant Three,
He was lazy, you will see.

Servant One gave his master the BIGGEST bag of money. The master was happy. Servant Two gave the master the BIG bag of money. The master was happy. Servant Three gave the master his SMALL bag of money. The master was not happy.

"You lazy servant!" shouted the master. "You did nothing with the money I gave you."

Servant One, Servant One,
Count on him to get things done.
Servant Two, Servant Two,
This man knew just what to do.
Servant Three, Servant Three,
He was lazy, you will see.

Jesus told this story to help people understand that God wants us to be responsible and do good things.

(Based on Matthew 25:14-29.)

© 1999 Abingdon Press.

The Angel's Message

by Peg Augustine

Have the children do the motions after you as suggested in the story.

The Story

Mary was a young girl who lived long ago in the little town of Bethlehem. Mary loved God and all the things God had made. (*Hold hands over heart.*) She liked to watch the sun come up in the morning (*bring arms over head to make a circle*) and go down at night. (*Bring arms down to sides.*) She liked to look at stars in the sky. (*Point to sky; look up.*) She liked to listen to the water in the stream near her house (*cup hands around ear*) and the birds singing in the trees. (*Cup hand around other ear.*)

An Angel Came
by Lorri Coates and Barbara McKone

An angel came to spread the joy . . .
(*Flap arms like wings.*)
Mary will have a baby boy.
(*Pretend to rock baby.*)
A child that comes from God above,
(*Raise arms above head; bring arms around and down at sides.*)
Born on earth to teach us love.
(*Hug yourself.*)

(Based on Luke 1:26-31.)

© 1998 Abingdon Press.

One day as Mary was thinking (*point to side of head*) about God's beautiful world, she heard a voice. (*Cup hand around ear.*) Looking up (*look up*), she saw an angel standing nearby. At first Mary was surprised and frightened! (*Hold hands up as if surprised.*) But the angel spoke to her in a soft voice, (*whisper*) "Don't be afraid, Mary. (*Shake head no.*) God is pleased with you.

"I have come to tell you a wonderful secret. (*Place fingers over lips.*) God is going to send you a baby boy. (*Pretend to rock baby.*) You will name him Jesus.

"He is God's own dear Son (*pretend to rock baby*), and he is God's greatest gift to the world. He will show everyone how to help one another and how to be happy together."

Mary listened to the angel (*cup hand around ear*), and her heart was filled with happiness. (*Put hands over heart.*) Her own little baby (*pretend to rock baby*) would grow up to help other people and to show them God's love. (*Put hands over heart.*)

Each day Mary thought about God's promise to her. (*Point to side of head.*) She sang a joyful song: "My soul praises the Lord (*raise arms above head*); and my heart is happy." (*Put hands over heart.*)

(Based on Luke 1:26-31.)

© 1997 Abingdon Press.

Teacher Talk

Christmas is Jesus' birthday.

Jesus was born in a stable in Bethlehem.

It's exciting to get ready for Christmas.

Jesus was once a baby, just as you were.

We thank God for Jesus.

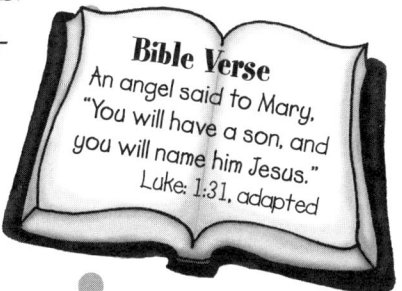
Bible Verse
An angel said to Mary, "You will have a son, and you will name him Jesus." Luke 1:31, adapted

Clippity Clop

by Daphna Flegal

Teacher Talk

We are happy at Christmas because it's Jesus' birthday.

Jesus was born in a stable in Bethlehem.

It's exciting to get ready for Christmas.

Jesus was once a baby, just as you were.

Bible Verse
An angel said to Mary, "You will have a son, and you will name him Jesus."
Luke: 1:31, adapted

Say: Before baby Jesus was born, Mary and Joseph had to go to Bethlehem. They packed the things they needed for the trip on a donkey. Let's pretend to be the donkey going with Mary and Joseph to Bethlehem. Each time you hear me say, "Clippity clop. Clippity clop," pat your hands on your legs to make the sound of a donkey walking.

Have the children practice patting their legs in an alternating pattern while you say, "Clippity clop. Clippity clop."

The Story

"Come, Mary," said Joseph. "We must go to Bethlehem. You can ride the donkey."

Clippity clop. Clippity clop. Joseph led the donkey to where Mary was waiting.

"It is a long trip to Bethlehem," said Mary. "We will need to take food and water." Mary put a bundle of bread and a jug of water on the donkey's back.

Clippity clop. Clippity clop. The donkey moved under the heavy load.

"We also must get ready for your baby," said Joseph. Joseph handed Mary the strips of cloth she would use to keep the baby warm.

Clippity clop. Clippity clop. The donkey was ready to go.

Joseph helped Mary sit on the donkey's back. He knew that Mary would soon have her baby.

Clippity clop. Clippity clop. The donkey started down the road to Bethlehem.

"Do you remember what the angel told us about the baby?" asked Mary.

"Yes," answered Joseph. "The angel told us to name the baby Jesus."

Clippity clop. Clippity clop. The donkey kept on walking to Bethlehem.

Soon Mary would have her baby. The baby's name was Jesus.

(Based on Luke 2:1-5.)

© 1997 Abingdon Press.

In the Stable
by Daphna Flegal

Animal Headbands

Materials needed: scissors, construction paper, crayons or markers, glue, tape

Photocopy the animal faces and cut out the ovals (see page 79). You will need one animal for each child. Cut construction paper into halves lengthwise to make strips. Let each child pick an animal face from the ovals. Encourage the children to decorate the animal faces with crayons or markers. Give each child two strips of construction paper. Have the child glue or tape the ends of the strips together to make one long strip. Show each child how to glue the animal face oval onto the strip. Measure the strip around each child's head so that the animal face is in the front. Tape the strip to make a headband.

Encourage the children to wear their animal headbands. Tell the children the story in a quiet voice. Have the children make the animal sounds with you.

The Story

Baa, baa. Baa, baa. The soft wooly sheep curled up on the hay.

Moo, moo. Moo, moo. The big brown cow closed her eyes.

Hee haw, hee haw. Hee haw, hee haw. The little grey donkey lay down.

Coo, coo. Coo, coo. The small gentle dove tucked his head under his wing.

It was nighttime. It was time for the animals to sleep in the stable.

Then something happened! A man and a woman came into the stable. It was Joseph and Mary. They had traveled a long way to get to Bethlehem. They were very tired, and it was time for Mary's baby to be born. Joseph made a bed for Mary in the soft hay.

Baa, baa. Baa, baa. The soft wooly sheep stood up.

Teacher Talk

We are happy at Christmas because it's Jesus' birthday.

Jesus was born in a stable in Bethlehem.

It's exciting to get ready for Christmas.

Jesus was once a baby, just as you were.

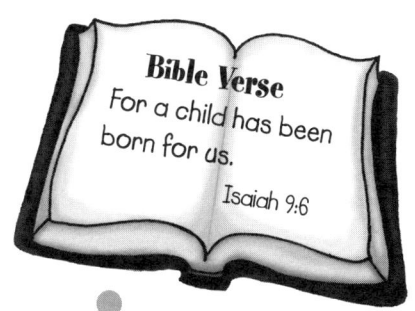

Bible Verse
For a child has been born for us.
Isaiah 9:6

Moo, moo. Moo, moo. The big brown cow opened her eyes.

Hee haw, hee haw. Hee haw, hee haw. The little grey donkey stood up.

Coo, coo. Coo, coo. The small gentle dove raised his head.

Waa, waa. Waa, waa. Baby Jesus was born in the stable that night. Mary wrapped baby Jesus in soft cloths. Joseph filled the manger with hay. Mary laid baby Jesus in the manger.

Baa, baa. Baa, baa. The soft wooly sheep looked in the manger.

Moo, moo. Moo, moo. The big brown cow sniffed at the manger.

Hee haw, hee haw. Hee haw, hee haw. The little grey donkey knelt next to the manger.

Coo, coo. Coo, coo. The small gentle dove flew down to sit on the side of the manger.

Mary sang a lullaby to baby Jesus.

Baa, baa. Baa, baa. The soft wooly sheep curled up on the hay.

Moo, moo. Moo, moo. The big brown cow closed her eyes.

Hee haw, hee haw. Hee haw, hee haw. The little grey donkey lay down.

Coo, coo. Coo, coo. The small gentle dove tucked his head under his wing.

Soon baby Jesus and the animals were fast asleep.

(Based on Luke 2:1-7.)

Copyright © 1999 Abingdon Press.

The Stable Song
words by LeeDell Stickler

Have the children sing the song below to the tune of "Little Cabin in the Woods."

Little stable in the town,
(Make a tent overhead with hands, fingertips touching.)
Bright starlight is shining down.
(Hold both hands up, fingers outstretched. Wiggle fingers as you bring arms down.)
Tiny baby, God's own Son,
(Pretend to rock a baby.)
Jesus is the One.
(Touch palm of left hand with middle finger of right hand; touch palm of right hand with middle finger of left hand. Then hold up index finger of right hand, indicating number one.)

(Based on Luke 2:1-7.)

Copyright © 1999 Abingdon Press.

(*Begin cutting the angel strip.*)

Then, out of the bright light, came the voice of an angel. "Don't be afraid," the angel said, "I have come to tell you something wonderful! Tonight in Bethlehem a baby was born, and this tiny baby is Jesus, God's Son. Get up and go to Bethlehem right now. The baby and his parents are resting in a stable. You will know him because he is sleeping in a manger."

(*Open up the angel strip.*)

Suddenly the sky was filled with angels singing, "Glory to God in heaven, peace has come to earth."

(*Set the angel strip on the floor.*)

The light went away, and the shepherds could not see the angels anymore. The shepherds all said to one another, "Let's go to Bethlehem and find the baby."

They hurried to Bethlehem and found the stable. Mary and Joseph were happy to have visitors. The shepherds knelt by the manger and looked at baby Jesus. They told Mary and Joseph what the angels had told them. Mary lifted her son from the manger and rocked him gently as she thought about the angel's song.

(*Pick up the sheep strip.*)

The shepherds went back to the field, where their sheep were still asleep. On their way the shepherds praised God for baby Jesus. They told everyone they passed the good news. Baby Jesus was born!

(Based on Luke 2:8-20.)

© 1997 Abingdon Press.

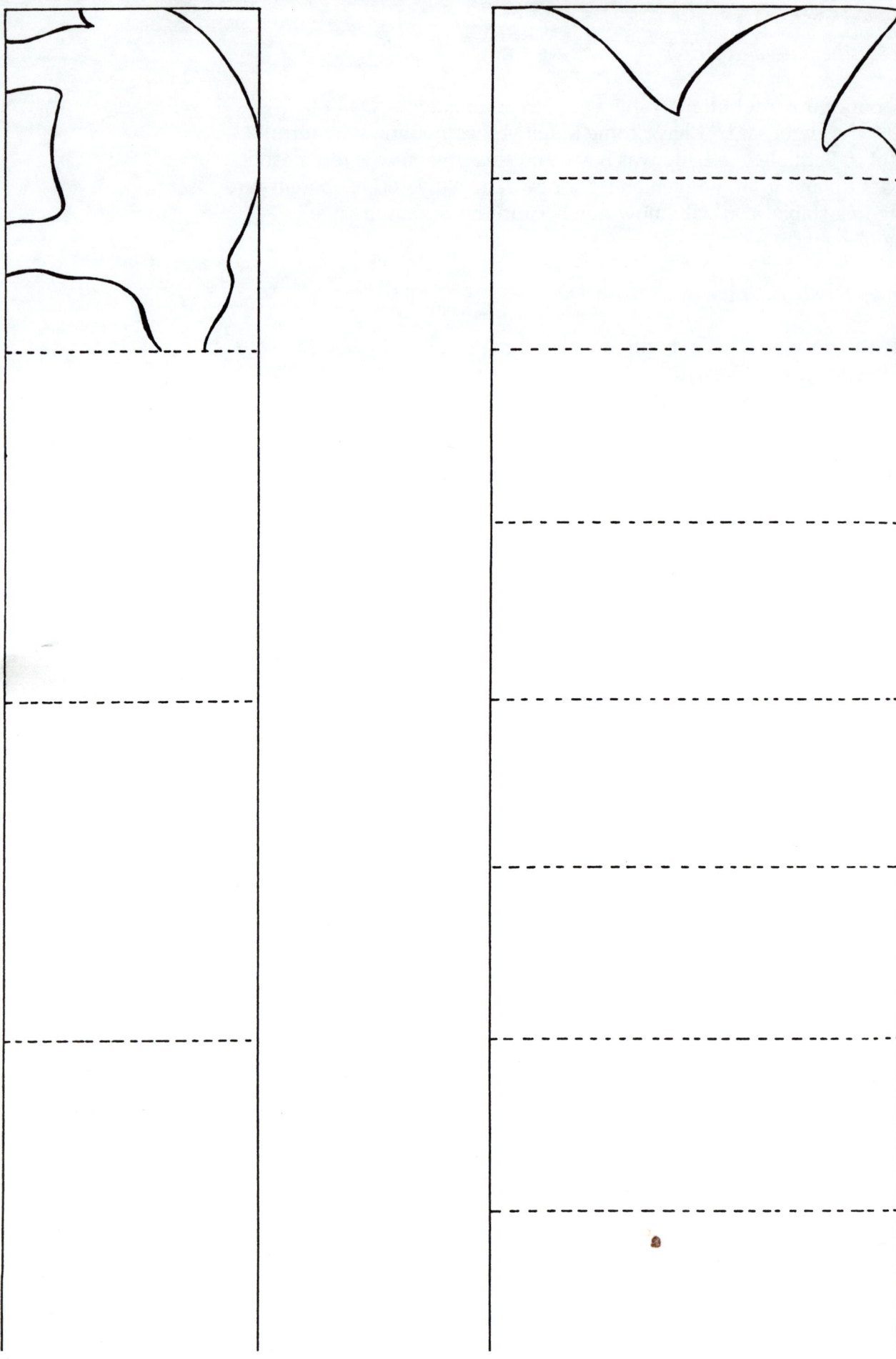

A Special Gift From God

by Daphna Flegal

Have the children stand in a circle. Encourage the children to do the motions with you as you tell the story. Or have a second teacher or helper do the motions as you tell the story.

The Story

Wait, wait, wait.
(*Cross arms over chest.*)
Simeon was waiting.
He was waiting to see a special gift from God.
(*Curl hands in front of eyes to make glasses.*)
Wait, wait, wait.
(*Cross arms over chest.*)
Simeon was waiting to see baby Jesus.
(*Pretend to rock a baby.*)

Wait, wait, wait.
(*Cross arms over chest.*)
Anna was waiting.
She was waiting to see a special gift from God.
(*Curl hands in front of eyes to make glasses.*)
Wait, wait, wait.
(*Cross arms over chest.*)
Anna was waiting to see baby Jesus.
(*Pretend to rock a baby.*)

Look, look, look.
(*Curl hands in front of eyes to make glasses.*)
See baby Jesus.
Mary and Joseph brought baby Jesus to the Temple.
(*Pretend to rock a baby.*)
Look, look, look.
(*Curl hands in front of eyes to make glasses.*)
Mary and Joseph thanked God for baby Jesus.
(*Pretend to rock a baby.*)

Teacher Talk

The Bible tells the story of Simeon and Anna.

Simeon and Anna knew that Jesus was a special gift from God.

We know that Jesus is a special gift from God.

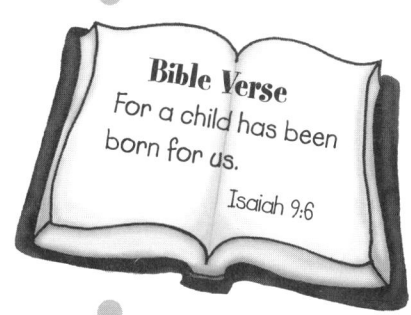

Bible Verse
For a child has been born for us.
Isaiah 9:6

Look, look, look.
(*Curl hands in front of eyes to make glasses.*)
Simeon saw baby Jesus.
Baby Jesus was the special gift from God.
(*Pretend to rock a baby.*)
Look, look, look.
(*Curl hands in front of eyes to make glasses.*)
Simeon thanked God for baby Jesus.
(*Pretend to rock a baby.*)

Look, look, look.
(*Curl hands in front of eyes to make glasses.*)
Anna saw baby Jesus.
Baby Jesus was the special gift from God.
(*Pretend to rock a baby.*)
Look, look, look.
(*Curl hands in front of eyes to make glasses.*)
Anna thanked God for baby Jesus.
(*Pretend to rock a baby.*)

Praise, praise, praise!
(*Shake hands above head.*)
Simeon and Anna praised God.
They were happy baby Jesus was born.
(*Pretend to rock a baby.*)
Praise, praise, praise!
(*Shake hands above head.*)
Simeon and Anna praised God for baby Jesus.
(*Pretend to rock a baby.*)

Praise, praise, praise!
(*Shake hands above head.*)
We can praise God.
We are happy baby Jesus is born.
(*Pretend to rock a baby.*)
Praise, praise, praise!
(*Shake hands above head.*)
We can praise God for baby Jesus.
(*Pretend to rock a baby.*)

(Based on Luke 2:22-38.)

© 1998 Abingdon Press.

Jesus Grew Just Like I Do

by Daphna Flegal

Lead the children in the following movement poem.

The Story

Response:
Jesus grew,
(*Put hands on hips. Touch right heel to the floor, then right toe.*)
Jesus grew,
(*Touch left heel to the floor, then left toe.*)
Jesus grew just like I do!
(*Touch toes; touch knees; touch shoulders; stretch arms above head.*)

When Jesus was a baby,
(*Rock baby.*)
He grew and grew and grew.
(*Crouch down; then stand on tiptoes.*)
He learned to crawl
(*Touch knees and hands to the floor.*)
Then learned to walk.
(*Walk in place.*)
He grew just like I do.
(*Touch toes; touch knees; touch shoulders; stretch arms above head.*)

(*Response*)

When Jesus was a little boy,
(*Point thumbs to shoulders.*)
He grew and grew and grew.
(*Crouch down; then stand up on tiptoes.*)
He learned to run
(*Run in place.*)
And learned to jump.
(*Jump in place.*)
He grew just like I do.
(*Touch toes; touch knees; touch shoulders; stretch arms above head.*)

(*Response*)

When Jesus was an older boy,
(*Hold hand above head to indicate height.*)
He grew and grew and grew.
(*Crouch down; then stand on tiptoes.*)
He learned to laugh
(*Hold stomach and shake.*)
And learned to sing.
(*Cup hands around mouth.*)
He grew just like I do.
(*Touch toes; touch knees; touch shoulders; stretch arms above head.*)

(Based on Luke 2:40.)

© 1997 Abingdon Press.

I Am Growing
by Susan Isbell

I am growing.
Look at me.
I can stretch up tall, you see.
I am growing.
Look at me.
I can touch the floor, you see.
I am growing.
Look at me.
I can stand on one foot, you see.
(Based on Luke 2:40.)
© 1997 Cokesbury.

Teacher Talk

Jesus grew from a baby to a boy.

God plans for you to grow.

Look at how much you have grown.

You can do many things.

Thank you, God, for all the ways we are growing.

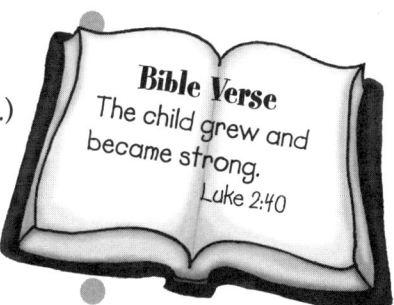

Bible Verse
The child grew and became strong.
Luke 2:40

Jesus in the Temple
by Peg Augustine

Teacher Talk

Jesus grew from a baby to a boy.

Jesus learned new things as he grew.

Jesus learned about God.

We can learn new things.

We can learn about God.

When Mary and Joseph search for Jesus in the story, ask the children the questions and let the children respond by shaking their heads and saying the response.

The Story

Once every year Mary and Joseph went to the Temple in Jerusalem to worship God. It was a long walk, but they loved the beautiful Temple, and they loved to worship God.

Jesus listened to the stories his parents told about the Temple. He wished he could go too. When he was twelve years old, his parents told him some wonderful news. He was old enough to go to the Temple with them!

Jesus and his family walked the long road to Jerusalem with a lot of other people. Jesus had a good time playing with his friends on the way. Finally they reached the city. For several days they went to worship in the Temple. All too soon it was time to go home. Mary and Joseph walked with the crowd of people back to Nazareth. They thought Jesus was walking with his friends.

When it was time to rest for the night, Mary and Joseph looked for Jesus. But Jesus was not with his friends. They started to worry. They were afraid something had happened to him. Leaving the crowd, Mary and Joseph walked back to Jerusalem looking for Jesus.

For two whole days they looked for Jesus, but they could not find him. First they looked for Jesus where the boys played ball in the marketplace.

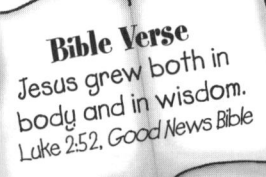

Bible Verse
Jesus grew both in body and in wisdom.
Luke 2:52, *Good News Bible*

Do you think Jesus was playing in the marketplace? No, Jesus was not in the marketplace. (*Shake head no.*)

Next they looked for him where the baker was putting bread into the big clay oven. Do you think Jesus was at the baker's? No, Jesus was not at the baker's. (*Shake head no.*)

Then they looked for Jesus where the women were getting water from the well. Do you think Jesus was at the well? No, Jesus was not at the well. (*Shake head no.*)

Finally on the third day Mary remembered how much Jesus had loved the Temple. Mary and Joseph hurried to the Temple.

Do you think Jesus was at the Temple? Yes, Jesus was at the Temple! (*Shake head yes*.)

He was sitting with the Temple leaders and teachers, listening and asking questions. The leaders and teachers were surprised to hear how much Jesus knew about God's love and God's plan for all God's children.

Mary hurried to Jesus and asked, "Son, why did you stay here? ~~Joseph~~ *Your Dad* and I have looked everywhere for you. We were frightened."

"I thought you would know where I was," Jesus said to Mary. "You know that my heart is filled with love for God and that I want to learn more about God."

Jesus slipped his hand into his mother's hand. As the family started back to their home in Nazareth, Mary thought about how much she loved Jesus.

(Based on Luke 2:41-52.)

© 1998 Abingdon Press.

The Big Catch
by Sharilyn S. Adair

Teacher Talk

The Bible tells the story of a man named Peter.

Peter was a fisherman.

Peter followed Jesus.

We can follow Jesus.

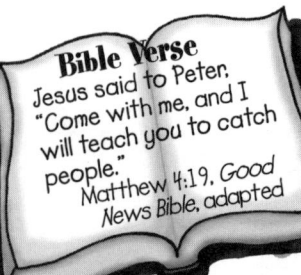

Bible Verse
Jesus said to Peter, "Come with me, and I will teach you to catch people."
Matthew 4:19, Good News Bible, adapted

Say: I need you to help me with some sounds and actions in today's story.

Have the children practice the following sounds and actions. Tell them to watch you in order to know when to do the sounds and actions in the story.

Splish-splash, splish-splash—Rub both hands back and forth together.
Tug! Pull! Tug! Pull!—Hold arms out in front of body; make hands into fists as though grasping a net and move arms toward body; repeat.
No fish—Shake head no.
Tweet! Tweet!—Say the words in a high-pitched voice.
Buzz-buzz!—Make a buzzing sound.

The Story

Stars twinkle in the sky as Fisherman Peter rows his boat out into the lake. Everything is quiet except for the sound of waves splashing against the boat. Fisherman Peter throws his net into the water and waits. **Splish-splash, splish-splash.** The waves rock Peter's boat. Peter is waiting for fish.

Tug! Pull! Tug! Pull! Fisherman Peter pulls his net back into the boat. Oh dear! **No fish.** Fisherman Peter rows to another part of the lake and throws out his net again. **Splish-splash, splish-splash.**

Tug! Pull! Tug! Pull! In comes the net. Does it have fish in it this time? **No fish.**

All night long Fisherman Peter throws out his net. **Tug! Pull! Tug! Pull!** Each time the net is empty. **No fish.**

Tweet! Tweet! Tweet! Tweet! Birds start to sing. The sun comes up. Fisherman Peter is tired. He rows to shore. He has no fish to sell. Fisherman Peter sees his friends James and John on the shore washing their nets. "I must wash my nets too," says Fisherman Peter.

What is that noise? **Buzz-buzz! Buzz-buzz!** The fishermen hear voices. **Buzz-buzz! Buzz-buzz!** The voices get louder. A crowd of people is coming toward the lake. Jesus is in the crowd. Jesus tries to talk to the crowd, but they are making too much noise. **Buzz-buzz! Buzz-buzz!**

Jesus sees Peter. "Peter, may I sit in your boat?" Jesus calls. "Yes," says Peter. Peter rows the boat out a ways. The crowd gets quiet. Jesus tells them that God loves and cares for them. Peter likes to listen to his friend Jesus. He doesn't feel so tired. Jesus finishes teaching about God, and the crowd goes away.

"Thank you, Peter, for letting me use your boat," says Jesus. "You need to catch some fish. Row out there. Throw your net out."

"Jesus, no fish are being caught. I have tried all night," says Peter. But he rows where Jesus tells him because Jesus is his friend.

Splish-splash, splish-splash. Waves splash against the boat again. Peter throws out his net.

Tug! Pull! Tug! Pull! Oh my! The net is so heavy that Peter cannot pull it in by himself. He waves to James and John to help. **Tug! Pull! Tug! Pull!** The fishermen empty the net into their boats.

Peter is surprised! There are more fish than Peter has ever caught before. He has lots of fish to sell.

(Based on Luke 5:1-11.)

© 2000 Abingdon Press.

Let's Go Fish
by Daphna Flegal

I'm a follower of Jesus.
You can be one too.
We can join our hands and follow.
Let's go fish!

Kind and loving just like Jesus,
That's the way to be.
If we really want to follow,
Let's go fish!

We can ask a friend to join us
And be loving too.
Jesus wants us all to follow.
Let's go fish!

A friend can ask a friend to join us,
And that friend can ask one too.
We can all join hands and follow.
Let's go fish!

We can ask more friends to join us.
Everyone can learn to love.
Jesus is the one we follow.
Let's go fish!

(Based on Luke 5:1-11.)

© 2000 Abingdon Press.

A Mighty Soldier

by Daphna Flegal

Teacher Talk

God plans for people to help us stay healthy.

God plans for people to help us when we are sick.

God is with us when we are sick and when we are well.

God is always with us.

Bible Verse
Heal the sick.
Matthew 10:8,
Good News Bible

Have the children stand in a circle. Tell the children the story and lead them in the motions for the refrain.

The Story

One day Jesus walked into a town. A soldier came to him.

There was a mighty soldier
(*Hold arms as if showing muscles.*)
Who ruled one hundred men.
(*Put fist of one hand on opposite shoulder.*)
He marched uphill;
(*March in place, raising up on tiptoes.*)
He marched downhill,
(*March in place, bending knees.*)
Then marched back home again.
(*March in place.*)

"Jesus," said the soldier, "my servant is sick."

"I will come to your house and make him well," answered Jesus.

There was a mighty soldier
(*Hold arms as if showing muscles.*)
Who ruled one hundred men.
(*Put fist of one hand on opposite shoulder.*)
He marched uphill;
(*March in place, raising up on tiptoes.*)
He marched downhill,
(*March in place, bending knees.*)
Then marched back home again.
(*March in place.*)

"Oh no," said the soldier. "You do not need to come to my house. Just say the word, and I know my servant will be well again."

"Go," said Jesus. "Your servant is now well."

The soldier went home. His servant was no longer sick. Jesus had made the servant well.

There was a mighty soldier
(*Hold arms as if showing muscles.*)
Who ruled one hundred men.
(*Put fist of one hand on opposite shoulder.*)
He marched uphill;
(*March in place, raising up on tiptoes.*)
He marched downhill,
(*March in place, bending knees.*)
Then marched back home again.
(*March in place.*)

(Based on Luke 7:2-10.)

Seeds
by Daphna Flegal

Have the children stand and do the motions for the repeating response. Then have the children sit down again.

The Story

One day Jesus walked to the seashore. He sat down beside the sea. Many people came to listen to Jesus teach about God. Soon there were so many people that no one could see Jesus. Jesus got into a boat floating on the water. Jesus sat in the boat while all the people stood on the seashore. Now the people could see Jesus. While Jesus was sitting in the boat, he told the people a story about a farmer and some seeds.

Response:
A farmer went into his field
To plant seeds in the ground.
He threw seeds here.
(*Pretend to throw seeds with one arm in a wide sweeping motion.*)
He threw seeds there.
(*Pretend to throw seeds with other arm in a wide sweeping motion.*)
He threw seeds all around.
(*Hold out both arms; turn around.*)

Some seeds fell on the road. Birds saw the seeds. They flew down and ate the seeds up.
(*Response*)

Some seeds fell among the rocks where there was not much dirt. Plants grew from these seeds, but there was not enough dirt to grow healthy roots. When the sun shone down on the plants, the plants got too hot and died.
(*Response*)

Some seeds fell among thorns. The plants grew, but the thorns grew faster. Soon the thorns choked the plants, and the plants died.
(*Response*)

Some seeds fell on good dirt. Many plants grew from the seeds. They grew and grew and grew!

Jesus told this story to help people understand that God loves us and wants us to share God's love with others.

(Based on Luke 8:5-8.)

© 1998 Abingdon Press.

Teacher Talk

Jesus told a story about a farmer who was planting seeds and about how the seeds grew.

God loves each one of us.

We can share God's love with others.

Bible Verse
God is love.
1 John 4:8

The Good Neighbor

by Daphna Flegal

Teacher Talk

You are important to God.

You are important to me.

God wants us to love other people.

Jesus told a story about a man who was a good neighbor.

We can be good neighbors.

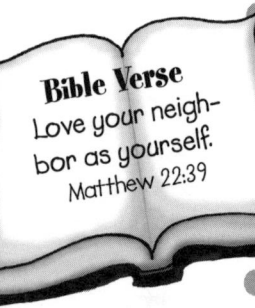

Bible Verse
Love your neighbor as yourself.
Matthew 22:39

Background and Storytelling Figures

Materials needed: crayons, scissors, tape or glue, drinking straws, box

Photocopy the background picture and storytelling figures (see pages 93-94). Have the children decorate the figures with crayons. Cut out the storytelling figures. Tape or glue a drinking straw on the back of each storytelling figure so that the straws come up from the figures' heads.

Let the children make a puppet theater. Cut flaps from a box or remove the box lid. Let the children decorate the background picture and box with crayons. Glue or tape the background picture inside the box. Place the theater where the children can see the background. Hold each story figure by the straw and do the actions mentioned in the story.

The Story

Jesus told people this story: Once there was a man traveling down the road to a town called Jericho. Suddenly robbers jumped out from behind some rocks. The robbers hurt the man and took the man's money. Then the robbers left the man and ran away.

Soon a priest came walking down the road. He saw the hurt man lying beside the road. He knew the man needed help, but he was afraid. He looked around to see if the robbers were still hiding nearby. The priest crossed the road and hurried by the hurt man. He did not stop to help.

Later a Levite, another leader from the Temple, came down the road. He saw the hurt man lying beside the road, but he did not want to touch the man. He crossed the road and hurried by. He did not stop to help.

Then a third man came riding down the road on his donkey. He was called a Samaritan. He saw the hurt man lying on the road. The Samaritan stopped to help the hurt man. He put the hurt man on his donkey and took him to a place where he could rest and get better. The Samaritan even paid for the hurt man's care.

Jesus looked at the people. "Three men saw the hurt man on the road," said Jesus. "Who was the neighbor to the man who was hurt?"

(Based on Luke 10:29-37.)

© 1998 Abingdon Press.

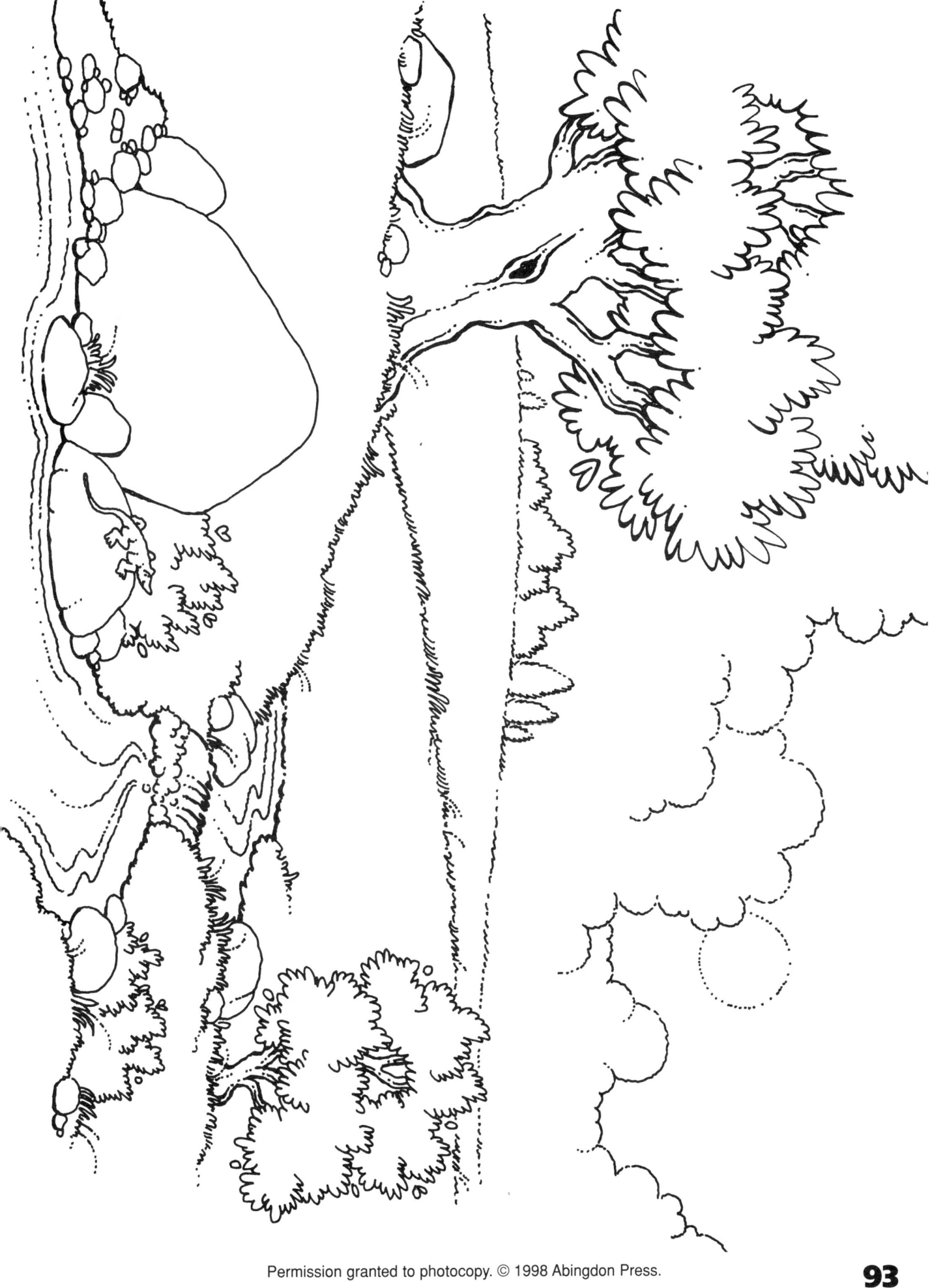

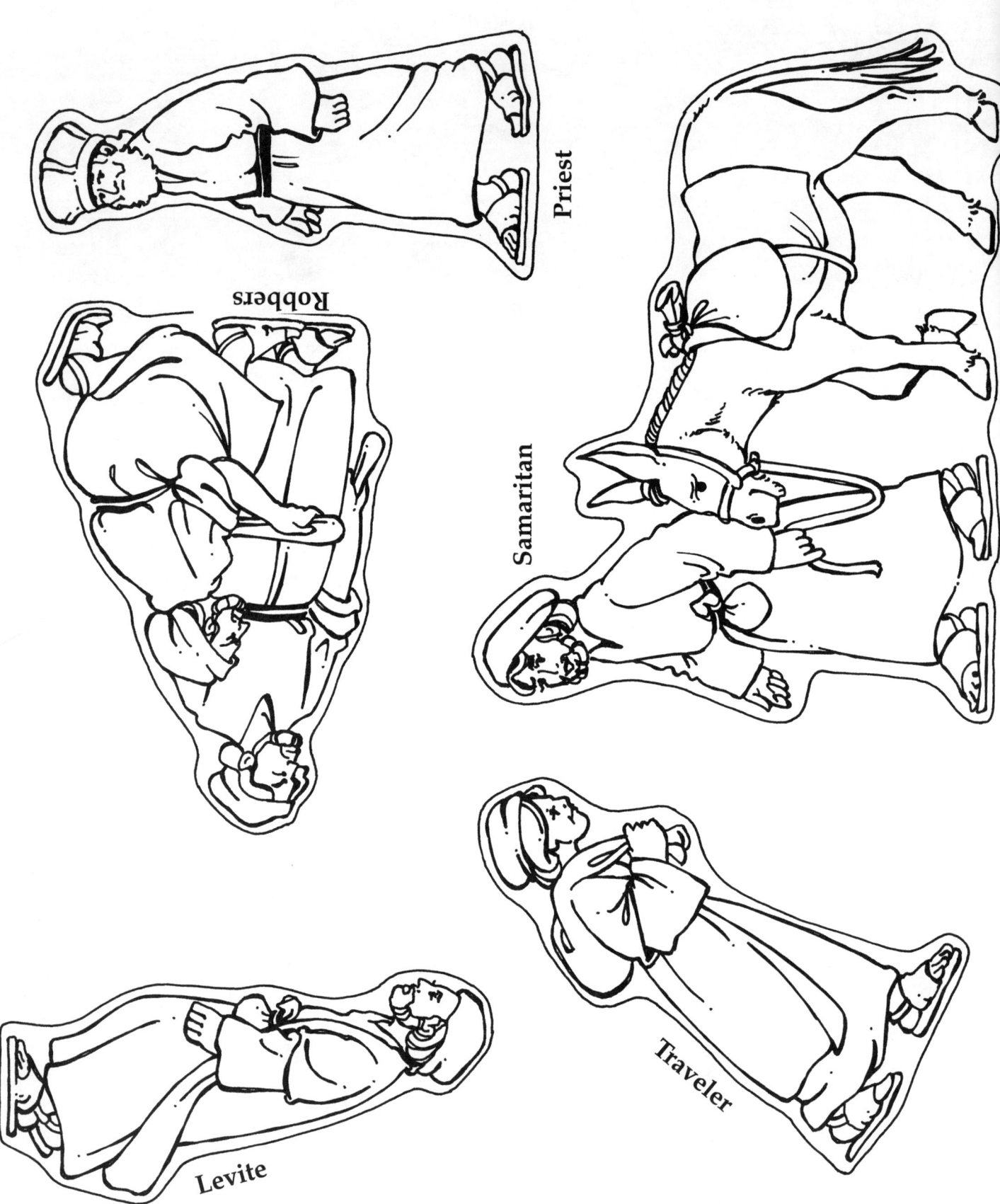

Listening to Jesus

by Susan Isbell

This story is an echo pantomime. Ask the children to listen carefully and to repeat each line after you say it.

The Story

Mary and Martha were sisters.
(*Open right hand for Mary, left hand for Martha.*)
They both loved Jesus very much.
(*Cross both hands over heart.*)
Mary and Martha were excited!
(*Open right hand for Mary, left hand for Martha.*)
Jesus was coming to their house.
(*Point to floor with both hands.*)

The day Jesus came, Martha stayed busy.
(*Hold hands up and shake both hands.*)
She cooked.
(*Stir a pot.*)
She cleaned.
(*Sweep.*)
She brought guests food.
(*Pretend to place food on table.*)

The day Jesus came, Mary sat quietly.
(*Put finger to lips to indicate quiet.*)
She listened to his stories.
(*Cup hand to one ear.*)
She listened to him teach.
(*Cup hand to other ear.*)
She listened as he told about God.
(*Cup hand to first ear again.*)

Martha became upset with Mary.
(*Put hands on hips.*)
"I have so much to do, and Mary won't help!"
(*Stomp foot.*)
Jesus smiled at Martha.
(*Smile.*)
"Listen!" Jesus said.
(*Cup both hands around ears.*)
"Come, sit, and listen.
(*Motion for someone to come toward you.*)
Mary is learning about God."
(*Sign God: Point index finger forward in front of you and draw your hand up. Draw your hand back down, opening the palm.*)
"Come, sit, and listen," Jesus said.
(*Motion for someone to come toward you.*)
"Listen and learn about God."
(*Sign God: Point index finger forward in front of you and draw your hand up. Draw your hand back down, opening the palm.*)

(Based on Luke 10:38-42.)

© 1996 Cokesbury.

© 1998 Abingdon Press.

Teacher Talk

The Bible tells us a story about two sisters named Mary and Martha.

Mary and Martha listened to Jesus.

Thank you, God, for our senses.

God plans for our ears to hear.

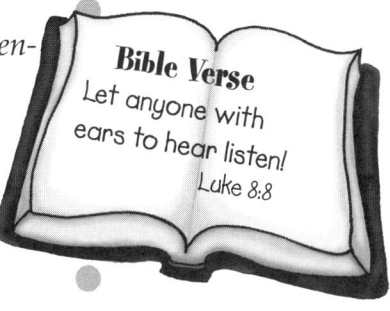

Bible Verse
Let anyone with ears to hear listen!
Luke 8:8

Fuzzy Wuzzy Was a...

by Daphna Flegal

Teacher Talk

You are important to God.

You are important to me.

Jesus told a story about a shepherd who cared for his sheep.

God loves you and every person in the world.

Sheep Mask

Materials needed: scissors, crayons or glue and packing peanuts or cotton balls, construction paper, tape

Photocopy and cut out a sheep mask (see page 97) for each child. Remember to cut out the eye holes. Let the children decorate the masks by coloring with crayons or by gluing on cotton balls or packing peanuts. Cut a two-inch-wide strip from construction paper for each child. Tape the strip to one side of the mask. Have each child hold the mask up to his or her face while you measure the strip around the back of the child's head. Tape the strip to the other side of the mask so that the mask will stay on the child's head. Encourage the children to move around the room and to pretend to be sheep.

Say: Come, little sheep; follow me. I am your shepherd. (*Lead the children around the room. Stop in one corner of the room.*) **Come and eat, little sheep; eat the sweet-tasting grass.** (*Lead the children to another area of the room.*) **Come and drink, little sheep; drink the cool water from the stream.** (*Lead the children to a rug or to your story area.*) **Now rest, little sheep; lie down and sleep in the warm sun.**

While the children are quiet, say the poem below.

The Story

Bible Verse
I am so happy I found my lost sheep. Let us celebrate!
Luke 15:6, *Good News Bible*

Fuzzy Wuzzy was a sheep;
He ate grass all day.
He drank water from the stream.
Then he'd run and play.

One day Fuzzy wandered off,
And he did not know where.
Fuzzy was afraid and lost,
Far from his shepherd's care.

The shepherd looked for Fuzzy
All day and all night long.
Finally, when he found the sheep,
He sang a happy song.

"Rejoice with me; my sheep
    was lost,
But now my sheep is found.
Fuzzy Wuzzy is back home.
My sheep are safe and sound."

(Based on Luke 15:4-7.)

© 1998 Abingdon Press.

Permission granted to photocopy. © 1998 Abingdon Press.

The Loving Father
by Susan Isbell

Teacher Talk

You are important to God.

You are important to me.

You are important to your family.

Families love and forgive each other.

Jesus told a story about a father and his two sons.

God always loves us, even when we make mistakes.

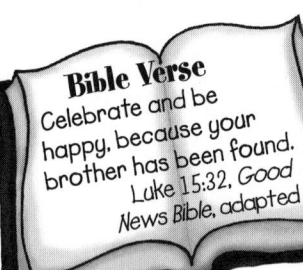

Bible Verse
Celebrate and be happy, because your brother has been found. Luke 15:32, *Good News Bible*, adapted

Pig Noses

Materials needed: scissors, crayons, glue or tape, construction paper

Photocopy and cut out the pig noses (see page 99). Let the children decorate the pig noses with crayons. Show each child how to fold the nose on the dotted lines. Glue or tape the flaps together. Cut construction paper into strips. Help each child glue or tape a construction paper strip to one side strip of the nose. Measure the strip around the child's head. Glue or tape the other end of the strip to the opposite side of the pig nose so that the nose fits comfortably around the child's head. Encourage the children to wear their pig noses.

Say: Today our Bible story is a story Jesus told about a father and his son. There are also pigs in the story. But the son did not like pigs. Having to take care of pigs made the son feel sad. When you hear me say the word *sad*, **pretend to be pigs and say, "Oink, oink." When you hear me say the word** *happy*, **clap your hands.**

The Story

Once upon a time there was a man who had two sons whom he loved very much. The two sons made the man very **happy**.

One day the younger son came to the father and said, "I am tired of living at home. Give me my share of the money now. I want to leave home." The father must have felt **sad**, but he gave the younger son the money.

The son was excited. He went to a country far, far away. He spent lots of money! He had lots of fun! He was **happy**!

But soon all his money was gone. He had no money for food. Alone and **sad**, the son finally found a job.

Oink! Oink! His job was feeding pigs. And he hated pigs! He didn't even want to touch the pigs. But he was so hungry, he would have been glad to eat the pigs' food. The son was very **sad**.

The son decided to go home. He wanted to tell his father he was sorry. He hoped his father would give him a job working in the fields. The son went back to his home. As he came near his house, he could not believe what he saw. His father was running down the road to meet him! The son was very **happy**!

"My son!" cried the father. "My son is home!" His father hugged him, kissed him, and welcomed him home. The father was very **happy**.

"Father, I'm sorry," said the son. "I have no money left. I made a mistake. What I did was wrong." The son felt **sad**.

"I love you, and I'm glad you are home," said the father.

The father planned a big party to welcome his son home. The father and the son were **happy**.

Jesus told this story so that people would know that God loves and forgives each of us, even when we make mistakes and do something wrong. Making mistakes can make us **sad**, but God's love can make us **happy**.

(Based on Luke 15:11-32.)

© 1994 Cokesbury.

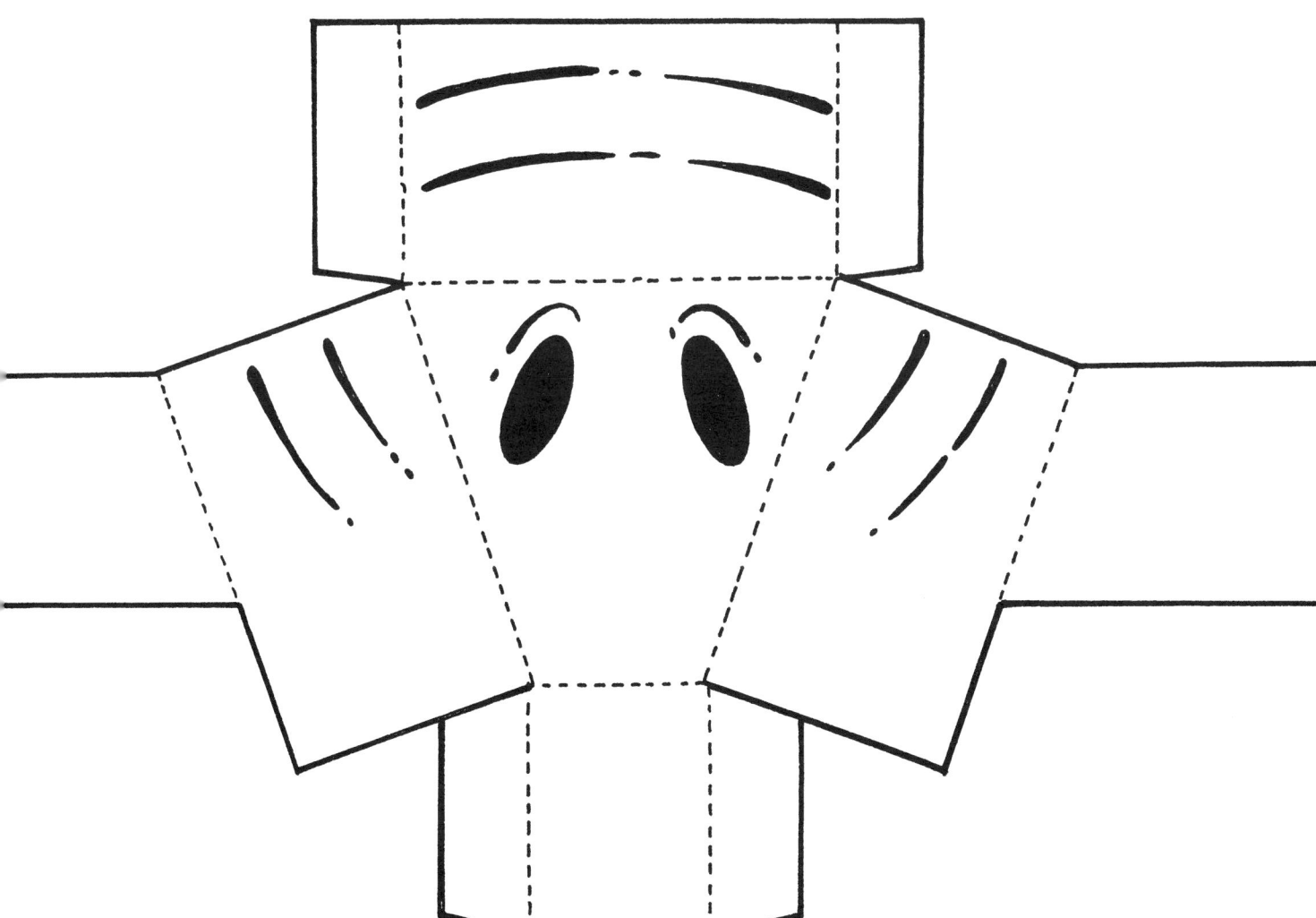

Permission granted to photocopy. © 1998 Abingdon Press

An Honest Man
by Daphna Flegal

Teacher Talk

The Bible tells the story of a man named Zacchaeus.

Zacchaeus was a tax collector.

Zacchaeus followed Jesus.

We can follow Jesus.

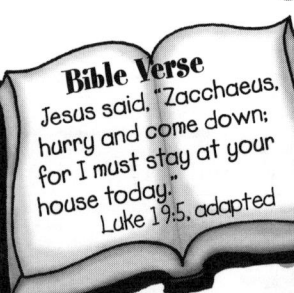

Bible Verse
Jesus said, "Zacchaeus, hurry and come down; for I must stay at your house today."
Luke 19:5, adapted

Coin Bags

Materials needed: crayons or markers; glue, tape, or stapler and staples; large play coins (optional: Bible-times costume)

Photocopy the coin bags (see page 101). Let the children decorate the bags with crayons or markers. Have the children fold the bags on the dotted lines. Help the children glue, tape, or staple the sides of the bags together to make an envelope. Write the children's names on their bags. Put at least four coins in each bag. Tell the story as if you were Zacchaeus, or ask another adult to dress up as Zacchaeus and tell the story. Zacchaeus needs to have at least four coins, as well as extra coins to give the children at the end of the story. Zacchaeus goes to each child and takes four of his or her coins when indicated in the story. At the end of the story Zacchaeus gives back five coins to each child.

The Story

My name is Zacchaeus. No one likes me. I don't have any friends. Do you know why? I'm a tax collector. I take money from people and give it to the Romans. But that's not all. I take more money than I should. Then I keep the extra money for myself. First I take coins for the Romans.

One, two for Rome. (*Count coins.*)

Then I take coins for me!

One, two for me! (*Count coins.*)

I know that is not honest, but I don't care! I see you have some coins. Have you paid your taxes?

One, two for Rome. (*Take two coins from each child.*)

One, two for me! (*Take two more coins from each child.*)

One day I heard that Jesus was coming to town. Crowds of people hurried into town to see him. I tried to see him, but there were too many people. I decided to climb a tree so that I could see.

Soon I saw Jesus. He smiled and waved to all the people. Then he walked right up to my tree.

He looked up and said, "Zacchaeus, hurry and come down, for I must stay at your house today."

I was so surprised, I almost fell climbing down the tree! I took Jesus to my house. He told me all about God. I listened to what Jesus said and decided right then to change my life.

I decided to give back all the money I had taken from the people. I even gave more than I had taken. I decided to be an honest man.

One, two, three, four, five for you! (*Give five coins back to each child.*)

(Based on Luke 19:1-8.)

© 1999 Abingdon Press.

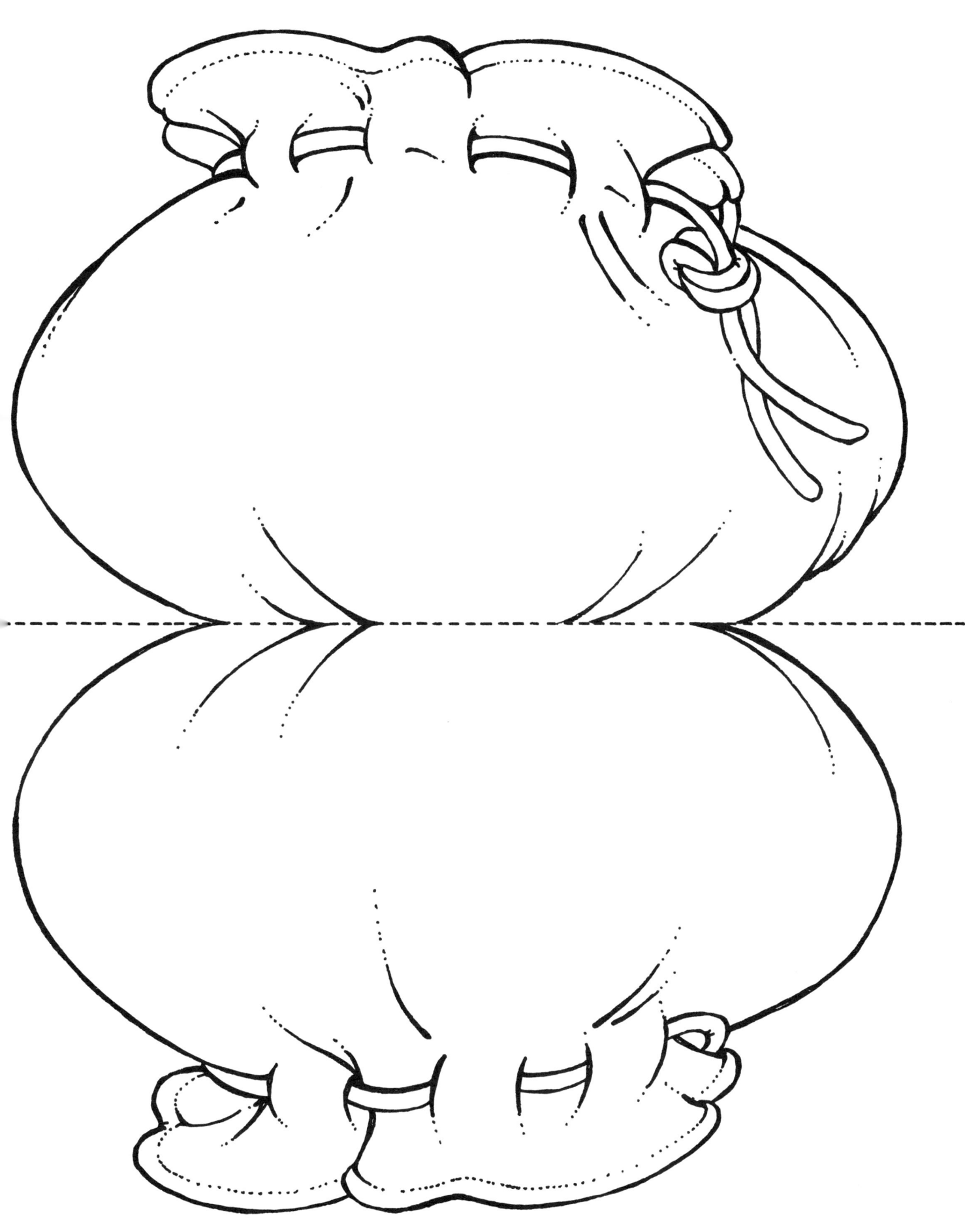

Two Coins
by Daphna Flegal

Teacher Talk

You are important to God.

You are important to me.

Jesus told a story about a woman who gave two coins in an offering to God.

God wants us to share with others.

Bible Verse
God loves a cheerful giver.
2 Corinthians 9:7

Materials needed: large play coins (fourteen for each child and twenty-one for the teacher), paper cups

Have the children sit down at a table. Place fourteen coins and a paper cup in front of each child. You will need twenty-one coins and a paper cup for yourself. Have the children count with you and drop their coins into their cups as indicated in the story.

The Story

One, two, three. (*Have each child drop three coins into the cup.*)

Jesus watched a rich man drop three coins into the offering box. He heard the sound the three coins made. Jesus knew he had more coins at home.

Clang, clang, clang. It was a loud sound.

One, two, three, four. (*Have each child drop four coins into the cup.*)

Jesus watched a rich woman drop four coins into the offering box. He heard the sound the four coins made. Jesus knew she had more coins at home.

Clang, clang, clang, clang. It was a loud sound.

One, two, three, four, five. (*Have each child drop five coins into the cup.*)

Jesus watched a rich man drop five coins into the offering box. He heard the sound the five coins made. Jesus knew he had more coins at home.

Clang, clang, clang, clang, clang. It was a very loud sound.

One, two. (*Have each child drop two coins into the cup.*)

Jesus watched a poor woman drop two coins in the box. He heard the sound the two coins made. Jesus knew she had no more coins at home.

Clang, clang. It was not a loud sound.

"This woman gave more than the others," said Jesus.

How can that be? (*Put two coins on the table or floor. Put three coins beside the two coins.*)

(*Count the two coins.*) One, two. (*Count the three coins.*) One, two, three. Two coins are less than three coins.

(*Add one more coin to the three coins. Count the two coins.*) One, two. (*Count the four coins.*) One, two, three, four. Two coins are less than four coins.

(*Add one more coin to the four coins. Count the two coins.*) One, two. (*Count the five coins.*) One, two, three, four, five. Two coins are less than five coins.

"This woman gave more," said Jesus, "because she gave all the coins she had."

(Based on Luke 21:1-4.)

© 1999 Abingdon Press.

Have You Heard the News?

Materials needed: shawl or scarf

Place a scarf or shawl over your head and pretend to be Mary as you tell the story. Or have another adult pretend to be Mary.

The Story

Have you heard the news? Have *you* heard the news? Did you know Jesus? Were you Jesus' friend? (*Ask each child a question.*) Come and listen. Let me tell you the most amazing thing.

My name is Mary. I'm a friend of Jesus. Today is Sunday. This morning another woman and I got up very early. We were going to the garden tomb. A tomb is a place where they bury people. Our best friend, Jesus, was dead. He was buried in the tomb. We felt very sad.

I can hardly believe what happened next! When we got to the tomb, Jesus was not there! That's right, the tomb was empty. We were so surprised! Then we noticed a young man sitting nearby. He said, "Jesus is not here. Jesus is alive!"

Can you imagine how we felt? We did not understand it, but we were very happy! We ran all the way back to the city. We found Jesus' other friends. We told them the good news. Jesus is alive!

Can you tell your friends the good news? Jesus is alive!

(Based on Luke 24:1-12.)

© 1992 Cokesbury.

Early in the Morning
by Daphna Flegal

It was early in the morning,
The first day of the week.
(*Hold up one finger.*)
A woman came to the garden tomb,
So sad, she began to weep.
(*Rub eyes as if weeping.*)
"Woman, why are you weeping?"
Said two angels sitting there.
(*Hold up two fingers.*)
"They've taken away my Lord," she said.
"And I do not know where."
(*Shake head no.*)
The woman turned and saw a man
Standing in the morning light.
(*Turn around.*)
At first she didn't know who he was.
Then she cried out with delight.
(*Cup hands around mouth.*)
The man standing there was Jesus.
She could hardly believe her eyes.
(*Point to eyes.*)
The woman ran to tell her friends,
"Jesus is alive!"
(*Raise arms in praise.*)
(Based on Luke 24:1-12; John 20:11-18.)
© 1998 Abingdon Press.

Teacher Talk

Easter is a special day to remember Jesus and his life.

Easter comes in spring.

Easter is a time to celebrate.

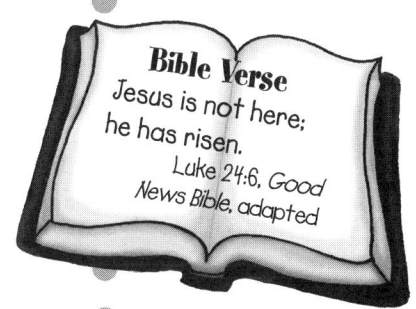

Bible Verse
Jesus is not here; he has risen.
Luke 24:6, *Good News Bible*, adapted

Mary, Mary

by Sharilyn S. Adair

Teacher Talk

The Bible tells a story about a woman named Mary.

You are important to God.

God loves you and cares about you.

God plans for people to take care of one another.

Bible Verse
Let love make you serve one another.
Galatians 5:13,
Good News Bible

Materials needed: crackers, softened cream cheese or peanut butter, lotion (all optional)

Have the children take off their shoes and socks and lie on their sides. (Do not force any child who does not want to take off his or her shoes and socks.) Jesus and his friends would have eaten a meal reclining in such an arrangement. Have the children follow your lead in acting out the following story. If possible, have another adult be Mary.

The Story

Let's pretend we are Jesus and his friends. We have been invited to Martha and Lazarus and Mary's house to eat a wonderful dinner. Martha cooked it, and it smells so good. (*Sniff the air.*) Can you smell the warm meat and the fresh-baked bread? Martha is such a good cook. Yum! I'm ready to eat, aren't you?

First, let's take off our shoes and socks. Then we can lie down around the table on our mats. Isn't this fun? This is how Jesus and his friends eat. They don't sit in chairs. Martha is putting the meat and vegetables in one large bowl on the table. We can rest on one elbow like this and use pieces of bread to help us eat the good meat juices in the bowl. Let's dip our bread pieces in the large bowl. Ooh! This food is so tasty, isn't it? Everyone, help yourself. (*This activity can be strictly pretend, or you can hand out crackers and have a dish of soft cream cheese or peanut butter in the center for the children to dip their crackers into.*)

Pretend that you are Jesus talking to your friend Lazarus. (*Rub lotion on the children's feet.*) Now you feel something soft and wet on your feet. Mary is rubbing perfume on your feet. Isn't that a loving thing to do? Now she is wiping your feet with her soft, soft hair. Doesn't it feel good? You think that Mary has done a kind thing to make your feet feel so good. And the smell of the perfume goes all over the room. Doesn't it smell good?

But Judas, another friend, is angry with Mary. He says she is wasting perfume. He says she could sell it for money to use to buy things for poor people. Mary's feelings are hurt. Let's shake our fingers at Judas for making Mary feel bad. We tell Judas that it is good to do things for people who are poor, but it is also good to show love to friends, and that's what Mary has done. She has done a kind thing.

Now our meal is over. We can put our shoes and socks on again.

(Based on John 12:1-8.)

© 1998 Abingdon Press.

A Change for Paul

by Daphna Flegal

Have the children say, "Love is kind" each time it appears in the story.

The Story

"All the followers of Jesus should be put in jail," Paul said angrily.

Paul was not a follower of Jesus. He did not know that **love is kind**.

"I'm going to stop the followers of Jesus from telling others about Jesus," Paul said. "I'm going to go to another city to look for followers of Jesus."

Paul was not a follower of Jesus. He did not know that **love is kind**.

Paul started down the road. Suddenly Paul saw a very bright light. Paul was so surprised, he fell to the ground.

"Paul, Paul," said a voice from the light. "Why are you unkind to people who follow me?"

"Who are you?" asked Paul.

"I am Jesus," said the voice. "Go to the city. I will send someone to teach you what I want you to do."

Paul listened to Jesus. He was learning that **love is kind**.

Paul stood up. He could not see anything. Some of his friends led him to the city. Paul stayed in the city three days.

A man named Ananias came to help Paul. "Paul, Jesus wants me to teach you how to be a follower of Jesus," said Ananias. He helped Paul see again.

Ananias helped Paul become a follower of Jesus. Paul learned that **love is kind**.

Paul made a change. He became a follower of Jesus. He told many, many people the good news about Jesus. Paul wrote letters that told people about Jesus' love.

Paul was a follower of Jesus. Paul knew that **love is kind**.

(Based on Acts 9:1-9, 17-18.)

© 1997 Abingdon Press.

Teacher Talk

The Bible tells the story of a man named Paul.

Paul taught people about Jesus.

We can tell people about Jesus.

Bible Verse
Love is kind.
1 Corinthians 13:4

A Busy Follower

by Sharilyn S. Adair

Teacher Talk

The Bible tells the story of a woman named Dorcas.

Dorcas made clothes for people.

Dorcas was a follower of Jesus.

We can follow Jesus.

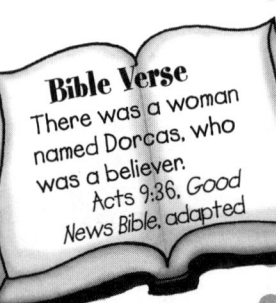

Bible Verse
There was a woman named Dorcas, who was a believer.
Acts 9:36, Good News Bible, adapted

Materials needed: Bible-times costumes, grocery-size paper bags

Get Bible-times robes, tunics, and headdresses from your Christmas pageant closet or gather dresses, bathrobes, shawls, and men's shirts that can pass as Bible-times garments. Put each garment into a separate bag. Have enough bags so that each child can hold one. Keep one yourself. Pass out the bags, but tell the children not to let anyone else see what is in their bags until they have a turn to do so.

The Story

Dorcas was a kind person. She was a follower of Jesus. She loved to sew, and the things she sewed always looked nice. Dorcas knew how to cut the cloth with her scissors to make different things to wear.

Snip! Snip! Snip! Her scissors would glide through the cloth. Then her busy fingers would push the needle in and out, in and out of the cloth until it became something to wear.

Sometimes when her scissors went snip, snip, snip and her fingers pushed the needle in and out, the cloth turned into a dress. Other times it was a coat to wear over the dress. And sometimes it was a long scarf for someone's head and shoulders. Dorcas was always busy. She made many, many dresses and coats and scarfs.

Dorcas made clothes to be a helper. She made clothes for people who did not have money to buy their own clothes.

Pretend that we are friends of Dorcas. Dorcas has made each of us something to wear. Let's take turns showing what Dorcas has made us and telling about it. I will start.

(Pull your garment out of the bag and hold it up for everyone to see. Talk about what it is. Show the children a hem so that they can see stitches. Talk about how Dorcas used a needle to make stitches. Let each child pull a garment out of his or her bag. Help the children describe each garment. Ask what color it is and whether it is a dress, a coat, or a scarf. If the children want to model the garments, let them do so. If you have a large class, use four or five bags and pull the garments out yourself, saying, "I wonder what could be in here. Is it a coat? Is it a dress? Is it a scarf? Let's see. Oh, it's a . . .")

My, Dorcas certainly was busy to make all of these fine things. What a good helper and follower of Jesus!

(Based on Acts 9:36-42.)

© 2000 Abingdon Press.

Lydia

by Daphna Flegal

Lydia Figure

Materials needed: block, plastic bottle, or cardboard tube; purple felt or purple fabric; tape; scissors

Photocopy and cut out the Lydia figure (see page 108) and tape it to a block, plastic bottle, or cardboard tube. Set the Lydia figure in the center of a piece of purple felt or purple fabric. Have the children follow the instructions in the story.

Say: Today our Bible story is about a woman named Lydia. Lydia sold purple cloth. She learned about Jesus.

The Story

Lydia sold purple cloth. Touch the purple cloth. Feel how soft it is? (*Have the children touch the purple cloth.*) Lydia liked the color purple. It was a special color. Only people who were rich could afford to buy purple cloth. Lydia was a rich and important person in the city of Philippi.

Lydia loved God. She prayed to God every day. Fold your hands as if you are saying a prayer. (*Have the children fold their hands in prayer.*) Lydia knew some other women who also loved God. They had no place to go in the city to pray to God, so Lydia and her friends met outside the city beside the river.

One day Lydia and her friends were sitting beside the river when a man named Paul came over to them. He told them all about Jesus. Lydia listened very carefully. (*Cup your hand around one ear.*) Show me how you listen carefully. (*Have each child cup a hand around one ear.*)

Lydia was happy to learn about Jesus. Show me how you look when you are happy. (*Have the children make happy faces.*) Paul baptized Lydia in the river, and she became a follower of Jesus. Lydia wanted her whole family to learn about Jesus. She invited Paul to stay at her house. Paul told Lydia's family about Jesus. Everyone at Lydia's house became a follower of Jesus.

Lydia still sold purple cloth. Touch the purple cloth again. (*Have the children touch the purple cloth.*) But now Lydia also helped others learn about Jesus.

(Based on Acts 16:11-15.)

© 1997 Abingdon Press.

Teacher Talk

The Bible tells the story of a woman named Lydia.

Lydia sold purple cloth.

Lydia welcomed Paul to her home.

Lydia learned about Jesus.

We can learn about Jesus.

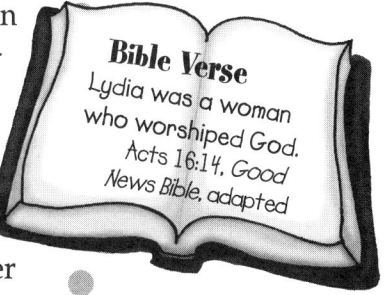

Bible Verse
Lydia was a woman who worshiped God. Acts 16:14, Good News Bible, adapted

A Love Letter

by Sharilyn S. Adair

Say: A man named Paul wrote a letter to a church. He told the people in the church all about love. His letter is in the Bible. I will tell you some things Paul said about love; then I will ask about some actions. If the actions do not show love, stamp your feet and say, "No! No! No!" If the actions do show love, clap your hands and say, "Yes! Yes! Yes!"

The Story

Love is patient. (*Clap hands and say, "Yes! Yes! Yes!"*)

Is love taking someone else's turn? (*Stamp feet and say, "No! No! No!"*) No, no! Love is patient. Love can wait. Love is happy for other people to have a turn.

Love is kind. (*Clap hands and say, "Yes! Yes! Yes!"*)

Is love pushing and shoving on the playground? (*Stamp feet and say, "No! No! No!"*) No, no! Love is kind. Love does not hurt anyone or make anyone feel bad.

Love is not jealous; love does not want what others have. (*Clap hands and say, "Yes! Yes! Yes!"*)

Is love crying because I want Timothy's bear? (*Stamp feet and say, "No! No! No!"*) No, no! Love is glad for others to have nice things. Love is thankful for my own things.

Love is not bragging; love does not think it is better than others. (*Clap hands and say, "Yes! Yes! Yes!"*)

Is love being glad that I am taller or can run faster than another child? (*Stamp feet and say, "No! No! No!"*) No, no! Love wants everyone to be happy.

Love is not selfish. (*Clap hands and say, "Yes! Yes! Yes!"*)

Is love showing off my new toys and not letting others play with them? (*Stamp feet and say, "No! No! No!"*) No, no! Love is sharing. Love wants everyone to have some.

Love does not have to have its own way. (*Clap hands and say, "Yes! Yes! Yes!"*)

Is love crying in the grocery store because Mother won't buy the cereal I want? (*Stamp feet and say, "No! No! No!"*) No, no! Love listens to others. Love knows that parents usually know what's best.

Love is happy about telling the truth. (*Clap hands and say, "Yes! Yes! Yes!"*)

Is love saying that someone else spilled the milk when I was the one? (*Stamp feet and say, "No! No! No!"*) No, no! Love never tells a lie.

Love never ends. (*Clap hands and say, "Yes! Yes! Yes!"*)

Jesus will always love us. (*Clap hands and say, "Yes! Yes! Yes!"*)

(Based on 1 Corinthians 13.)

© 1999 Abingdon Press.

Teacher Talk

I love you!

I want you to be loving toward your friends.

God loves you!

People in Bible times wrote letters.

We write letters today.

Mail carriers help us send letters.

We thank God for mail carriers.

Bible Verse
Love is kind.
1 Corinthians 13:4

Christ Strengthens Me

Teacher Talk

God is with us when things are hard.

God wants to helps us when things are hard.

Thank you, God, for being there when we need you.

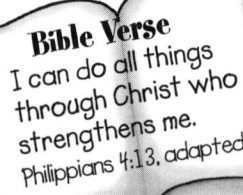
Bible Verse
I can do all things through Christ who strengthens me.
Philippians 4:13, adapted

(Based on Philippians 4:13.)

© 2000 Abingdon Press.

Index by Scripture

Genesis
Genesis 1:1-5 - "God Created Day and Night" 8
Genesis 1:1-5 - "The Sun and the Moon" 8
Genesis 1:6-10 - "It Is Good, It Is Good" 9
Genesis 1:11-13 - "God Created Seeds" 10
Genesis 1:14-19 - "Sun, Moon, Stars" 11
Genesis 1:20-23 - "All Kinds of Creatures" 13
Genesis 1:20-23 - "God Made Things That Fly " 14
Genesis 1:24-25 - "God Created Animals" 15
Genesis 1:26-27 - "In God's Image" 16
Genesis 1:1-31 - "The Bible Tells Me" 16
Genesis 2:7-8, 21-22 - "Adam and Eve" 17
Genesis 2:7-8, 21-22 - "Adam 'n Eve March" 17
Genesis 2:18-20 - "Naming the Animals " 19
Genesis 6:9, 14-16; 7:1-18; 9:13-15 - "Noah's Very Big Boat" 21
Genesis 6:19-20 - "Two by Two" 22
Genesis 28:10-17 - "Dream, Dream, Dream" 23
Genesis 28:15 - "God Is With Me" 24
Genesis 37:17-32; 41:39-57; 45:4-5 - "The New Coat" 26
Genesis 41:39-57; 45:4-5 - "Joseph Shows Love" 29

Exodus
Exodus 2:1-10 - "Sister Miriam Watched" 30
Exodus 2:1-10 - "Who Has the Baby?" 31
Exodus 2:1-10 - "Little Baby Moses" 33
Exodus 20:1-17 - "Respect Your Parents" 34
Exodus 25:1-9 - "A Special Place of Worship" 38
Exodus 25:1-9 - "Moses, Moses" 38

Ruth
Ruth 1–4 - "Ruth: A Story of God's Love" 39

Samuel
Samuel 18:1-4 - "Very Good Friends" 40
Samuel 18:1-4 - "Special Friends" 40

Esther
Esther 2–8 - "Queen Esther, Queen Esther" 41

Psalms
Psalm 8; Genesis 1:1-31 - "God Is Good" 42
Psalm 9:1; Genesis 1:1-31 - "Wonderful Things" 43
Psalm 9:1 - "Clap Your Praise" 43
Psalm 23 - "Come, Little Sheep" 44
Psalm 23 - "God Is Like a Shepherd" 45
Psalm 34:8 - "O Taste and See" 47
Psalm 100 - "Worship the Lord With Joy" 48
Psalm 149 - "Sing a New Song" 49
Psalm 149 - "Sing Praise to God" 49
Psalm 150 - "Praise the Lord" 50
Psalm 150 - "Praise God!" 51

Proverbs
Proverbs 17:17 - "Be a Friend" 53

Ecclesiastes
Ecclesiastes 3:1 - "For Everything There Is a Season" 54
Ecclesiastes 3:1; Genesis 8:22 - "The Seasons" 55

Jonah
Jonah 1–2 - "An Echo Fish Story" 56

Matthew
Matthew 2:1-12 - "Twinkle, Twinkle" 58
Matthew 2:1-12 - "Look!" 59
Matthew 5:1-12 - "Happy Teachings" 61
Matthew 6:9-13 - "Talking to God" 63
Matthew 6:9-13 - "Amen, Amen, Amen" 64
Matthew 6:25-34 - "God Cares" 66
Matthew 6:25-34 - "Let's Pretend" 66
Matthew 8:14-15 - "Jesus Heals Peter's Mother-in-law" ... 67
Matthew 13:31-32 - "Little and Big" 69
Matthew 8:23-26 - "The Big, Big Windstorm" 70
Matthew 14:15-21 - "Count and Chant" 72
Matthew 25:14-29 - "Three Servants" 74

Luke
Luke 1:26-31 - "The Angel's Message" 75
Luke 1:26-31 - "An Angel Came" 75
Luke 2:1-5 - "Clippity Clop" 76
Luke 2:1-7 - "In the Stable" 77
Luke 2:1-7 - "The Stable Song" 78
Luke 2:8-20 - "The Shepherds" 80
Luke 2:22-38 - "A Special Gift From God" 83
Luke 2:40 - "Jesus Grew Just Like I Do" 85
Luke 2:40 - "I Am Growing" 85
Luke 2:41-52 - "Jesus in the Temple" 86
Luke 5:1-11 - "The Big Catch" 88
Luke 5:1-11 - "Let's Go Fish" 89
Luke 7:2-10 - "A Mighty Soldier" 90
Luke 8:5-8 - "Seeds" 91
Luke 10:29-37 - "The Good Neighbor" 92
Luke 10:38-42 - "Listening to Jesus " 95
Luke 15:4-7 - "Fuzzy Wuzzy Was a . . ." 96
Luke 15:11-32 - "The Loving Father" 98
Luke 19:1-8 - "An Honest Man" 100
Luke 21:1-4 - "Two Coins" 102
Luke 24:1-12 - "Have You Heard the News?" 103
Luke 24:1-12; John 20:11-18 - "Early in the Morning" 103

John
John 12:1-8 - "Mary, Mary" 104

Acts
Acts 9:1-9, 17-18 - "A Change for Paul" 105
Acts 9:36-42 - "A Busy Follower" 106
Acts 16:11-15 - "Lydia" 107

1 Corinthians
1 Corinthians 13 - "A Love Letter" 109

Philippians
Philippians 4:13 - "Christ Strengthens Me" 110

Index by Subject

The Beatitudes
"Happy Teachings" 61

Creation
"God Created Day and Night" 8
"The Sun and the Moon" 8
"It Is Good, It Is Good" 9
"God Created Seeds" 10
"Sun, Moon, Stars" 11
"All Kinds of Creatures" 13
"God Made Things That Fly " 14
"God Created Animals" 15
"In God's Image" 16
"The Bible Tells Me" 16
"Adam and Eve" 17
"Adam 'n Eve March" 17
"Naming the Animals" 19
"For Everything There Is a Season" 54
"The Seasons" 55

111

David
"Very Good Friends" 40
"Special Friends" 40
"Come, Little Sheep" 44
"God Is Like a Shepherd" 45

The Early Church
"A Change for Paul" 105
"A Busy Follower" 106
"Lydia" 107
"A Love Letter" 109
"Christ Strengthens Me" 110

Esther
"Queen Esther, Queen Esther" 41

Friendship
"Be a Friend" 53

Jacob
"Dream, Dream, Dream" 23
"God Is With Me" 24

Jesus As a Child
"Jesus Grew Just Like I Do" 85
"I Am Growing" 85
"Jesus in the Temple" 86

Jesus' Birth
"A Special Gift From God" 83
"The Angel's Message" 75
"An Angel Came" 75
"Clippity Clop" 76
"In the Stable" 77
"The Stable Song" 78
"The Shepherds" 80
"Twinkle, Twinkle" 58
"Look!" 59

Jesus' Ministry
"The Big, Big Windstorm" 70
"The Big Catch" 88
"Fuzzy Wuzzy Was a . . ." 96
"God Cares" 66
"The Good Neighbor" 92
"Jesus Heals Peter's Mother-in-law" 67
"Let's Go Fish" 89
"Let's Pretend" 66
"Listening to Jesus " 95
"Little and Big" 69
"The Loving Father" 98
"Mary, Mary" 104
"A Mighty Soldier" 90
"Seeds" 91
"Three Servants" 74
"Two Coins" 102

Jesus' Resurrection
"Have You Heard the News?" 103
"Early in the Morning" 103

Jonah
"An Echo Fish Story" 56

Joseph
"The New Coat" 26
"Joseph Shows Love" 29

Loaves and Fishes
"Count and Chant" 72

The Lord's Prayer
"Talking to God" 63
"Amen, Amen, Amen" 64

Moses
"Sister Miriam Watched" 30
"Little Baby Moses" 33
"Moses, Moses" 38
"Who Has the Baby?" 31
"A Special Place of Worship" 38
"Respect Your Parents" 34

Noah
"Noah's Very Big Boat" 21
"Two by Two" 22

Psalms
"God Is Good" 42
"The Book of Psalms" 42
"Clap Your Praise" 43
"Wonderful Things" 43
"O Taste and See" 47
"Worship the Lord With Joy" 48
"Sing a New Song" 49
"Sing Praise to God" 49
"Praise the Lord!" 50
"Praise God!" 51

Ruth
"Ruth: A Story of God's Love" 39

Zacchaeus
"An Honest Man" 100

Reproducible Art Index

Sun, Moon, and Stars (Creation) 12
Garden Picture (Garden of Eden) 18
Animal Pictures (Creation) 20
Angels (Jacob's Ladder) 24
Jacob's Ladder 25
Robe Shaker (Joseph's Coat) 28
Moses' Basket 32
Numbers (Ten Commandments) 36-37
Sheep Puppet (Psalm 23) 46
Tambourine Picture (Psalm 150) 52
Starscope (The Wise Men's Visit) 60
Happy Stick (The Beatitudes) 62
Prayer Square (The Lord's Prayer) 65
Hot 'n Happy Hat (Jesus Heals) 68
Fish and Bread Pictures 73
Animal Headbands (Jesus' Birth) 79
Angel and Sheep Strips (Jesus' Birth) 82
Background Picture (Good Samaritan) 93
Storytelling Figures (Good Samaritan) 94
Sheep Mask (The Lost Sheep) 97
Pig Nose (The Loving Father) 99
Coin Bag (Zacchaeus) 101
Lydia Figure 108